THE EXECUTION OF THE HANGMAN OF RIGA

'ANTON KUENZLE'
GAD SHIMRON

THE EXECUTION OF THE HANGMAN OF RIGA

THE ONLY EXECUTION OF A NAZI WAR CRIMINAL BY THE MOSSAD

Translated from the Hebrew by

URIEL MASAD

Edited and with an introduction by

SHLOMO J. SHPIRO

VALLENTINE MITCHELL
LONDON • PORTLAND, OR

First published in 2004 in Great Britain by
VALLENTINE MITCHELL
Suite 314, Premier House,
112–114 Station Road,
Edgware, Middlesex, MA8 7BJ

and in the United States of America by
VALLENTINE MITCHELL
c/o International Specialized Book Services, Inc.,
920 NE 58th Avenue, Suite 300
Portland, Oregon, 97213-3786

Website: www.vmbooks.com

Previously published in Hebrew by Keter and in German by Bleicher Verlag

Translated from Hebrew by Uriel Masad

British Library Cataloguing in Publication Data
Kuenzle, Anton
The execution of the hangman of Riga: the only execution of a Nazi war criminal by the Mossad
1. Cukurs, Herberts – assassination 2. Keunzle, Anton 3. Israel. Mossad le-modiin ve-tafkidin meyuhadim 4. War criminals – Latvia 5. Fugitives from justice – Uruguay
I. Title II. Shimron, Gad
364.1′51′092

ISBN 0-85303-533-4 (cloth)
ISBN 0-85303-525-3 (paper)

Library of Congress Cataloging-in-Publication Data
Künzle, Anton, 1919 –
[Hisul ha-talyan me-Riga. English]
The execution of the hangman of Riga: the only execution of a Nazi war criminal by the Mossad/'Anton Kuenzle', Gad Shimron; translated from the Hebrew by Uriel Masad.
p. cm.
ISBN 0-85303-533-4 (cloth) – ISBN 0-85303-525-3 (pbk)
1. Cukurs, Herbert, 1900–1965. 2. War criminals–Latvia–Råga. 3. Jews–Persecutions–Latvia–Råga. 4. Holocaust, Jewish (1939–1945)–Latvia–Råga. 5. Nazis–Brazil. 6. Nazis–Uruguay–Montevideo. 7. Kènzle, 1919– I. Shimron, Gad, 1950–II. Title.

D804.L35K8613 2004
364.15′1′092–dc22

2003066555

Typeset by FiSH Books, London
Printed in Great Britain by MPG Books Ltd, Bodmin, Cornwall

With gratitude to my wife who, throughout our many years together, the good times and the hard, often on her own and in the dark, was my true friend and companion, my support and the keeper of our family, thus enabling me to do what I considered to be my duty.

'Anton Kuenzle'

Yizkor – In Memoriam

In memory of the Jews of Riga who were killed in the Holocaust by the murderers, devout pupils and abettors of the Nazi beast.

In memory of my parents, decent and honest people, who healed and helped so many people throughout their lives before disappearing without a trace in the Theresienstadt and Auschwitz concentration camps in the Holocaust.

CONTENTS

ACKNOWLEDGEMENT

The authors wish to thank Dr Ady Tzidon for introducing them to Vallentine Mitchell Publishers.

LIST OF ILLUSTRATIONS

(between pages 72 and 73)

FOREWORD

THE GREATEST Holocaust in history, which took place in Europe under the Nazi regime and resulted in the killing of over six million Jews, was a unique event in every sense. After the Second World War, only a few of the Nazi criminals were put on trial before an international tribunal. Many of the wanted war criminals managed to escape and create new lives for themselves – the most popular place of refuge was South America. In those far-off countries, war criminals immersed themselves in the local population and managed to survive.

The State of Israel decided not to neglect this matter and to eliminate the leading criminals. This was not a broad, no-holds-barred operation but rather a targeted, selective and efficient elimination. The most widely known case was the capture of Adolf Eichmann, who organized the machinery of the Holocaust. Eichmann was captured in Argentina and brought to trial in Israel.

However, Eichmann was not the only one. Other people whose crimes were proven were also targets for elimination. One of the most prominent in that group was Herbert Cukurs, a criminal who wrought disaster on the Jews of Latvia. Cukurs, known as the 'Hangman of Riga', escaped from the Allies and found refuge in Brazil. This book describes in a detailed and poignant way a truly successful Israeli intelligence operation which placed Cukurs in his coffin.

The hero of this book uses the pseudonym 'Anton Kuenzle', in order to conceal his true identity. Once Cukurs was located in Brazil, Kuenzle was ordered to befriend him and bring him to another South American country, Uruguay, where a suitable place was prepared to eliminate him. There, in a small country house distant from centres of population, the hit squad headed by the commander of the Israeli Mossad's operational unit was assembled.

Kuenzle succeeded admirably in identifying with his assigned role and, under the cover of a rich businessman who had come to South America to make large investments, lured Cukurs into the trap. This operation is told by Kuenzle in the first person, in simple and clear words. It is an incredible story of a complex scheme hatched by an Israeli intelligence officer which turned into a close relationship with his target. This friendship undoubtedly helped settle the score with Cukurs.

Kuenzle already had extensive security and business experience. He served in the British Army during the Second World War. When the State of Israel was founded, he enlisted in the Israel Defence Forces (IDF) and served in different combat units and later in the artillery, where he climbed through the ranks to be appointed Commander of the Artillery School. In the early 1960s, he joined the intelligence community and performed a range of duties in the Mossad, including spending many years abroad and in training.

Kuenzle succeeded so well in his career because he possessed several basic traits which characterize a good intelligence officer. First, he had the look of an innocent person whom nobody could suspect of any covert activities. Second, he acquired extensive skills through his wide operational experience. Third, he is a cool and composed person who does not lose his wits and always finds a solution to complicated problems. This was Kuenzle and those were the reasons for the success of this operation.

All in all, we have before us a fascinating book, based on real facts – a classic case of truth being stranger than fiction.

General Meir Amit
Head of the Mossad, 1963–68

INTRODUCTION

THE STATE of Israel, established in May 1948, was founded as a national home for the Jewish people. Only three years previously, the end of the Second World War and the liberation of the concentration camps had exposed the terrible crimes of the Nazi regime against the Jews. Six million Jews fell victim to the Nazi 'Final Solution', their systematic plan to exterminate the Jewish people. Those few saved from the gas chambers were put into Displaced Persons (DP) camps across Europe. In November 1947 the United Nations decided that Palestine, then under British Mandate rule, should be divided into two states, one Jewish and one Arab. The small Jewish population in Palestine declared its independence and the new state committed itself to serve as a secure home for the survivors of Nazi genocide. When Prime Minister David Ben-Gurion declared statehood, he stated that Israel would never forget either the victims of the Holocaust nor the crimes of their Nazi torturers. In this vein, the State of Israel perceived itself as representing the entire Jewish people when it took upon itself the mission to prosecute Nazi war criminals. One of the first statutes enacted by the Knesset, the Israeli Parliament, became known as the 'Law for Bringing to Justice Nazi Criminals and their Collaborators'. It is the only statute in Israel's law books that carries the death sentence. It is this commitment that formed the background for Israeli intelligence activities against Nazi war criminals throughout the world.

The Execution of the Hangman of Riga is the story of an operation carried out by Israel's foreign intelligence service, the Mossad, to identify, locate and execute the notorious Nazi criminal, Herbert Cukurs. The main part of the operation was carried out almost single-handedly by one of the

Mossad's top agents, an exceptional intelligence operative with extensive experience in undercover missions. 'Anton Kuenzle' was the cover name used by the Mossad agent for the Cukurs operation. His real name must remain secret for security reasons.

This book is a unique manuscript. It is the first time that a former Mossad agent has revealed in detail the inner workings of an execution, and it provides an in-depth look into the world of real intelligence, not the fiction often presented by the popular media. In a clear and self-depreciating manner, Kuenzle describes how he planned and carried out this risky operation alone, how he created an identity aimed at enticing Cukurs away from his secure life in Brazil into a trap laid for him in Uruguay. Through his unique ability to inspire confidence, Kuenzle quickly befriended Cukurs, becoming a family friend and developing the prospect of lucrative business connections with Cukurs, who came to trust him totally. Cukurs was lured to Uruguay through the promise of a profitable deal. There he met his fate at the hands of a Mossad hit team. The Nazi war criminal paid the ultimate price for his horrifying crimes against humanity.

Anton Kuenzle is a remarkable person. Walking down the street of almost any Western capital, he would not stand out as a dashing James Bond character. With thinning hair and a slight paunch, he looks just like thousands of other citizens going about their daily business. However, Kuenzle possesses a unique talent, desperately sought after by intelligence services – the ability to blend into his surroundings in almost any situation. Known as 'the man with the hundred identities', Kuenzle travelled around the world on Mossad missions, under numerous covers. His ability to identify himself completely with his cover identity, combined with a natural ability to convey trustworthiness, made his cover faultless. Once he obtained false papers declaring him to be someone else, it was as though he underwent a complete identity transformation, becoming wholly absorbed in the identity he acquired. Yet at the end of a mission he was just as easily able to return to his real life and family in Israel.

Kuenzle was born in Germany. His father, a well-known physician and a proud German, was awarded the Iron Cross in the First World War. His mother, a language teacher, instilled in the young Anton the ability to learn new languages quickly. As a child Kuenzle studied Latin, Greek and French, language skills that were put to good use later as he travelled the world. As a young adolescent, Kuenzle witnessed the rise of the Nazi regime in Germany and the ensuing wave of anti-Semitism, which engulfed every aspect of life. A year after Hitler's rise to power, in 1934, the 15-year-old Kuenzle left Germany alone to make a new life in Palestine.

Kuenzle attended high school in Palestine, where he met many of the friends who were to accompany him in later life. He was committed to security issues and in 1936, as Arab rioters attacked Jewish settlements in Palestine, he became a member of the Hagana, the underground Jewish militia formed to defend the Jewish population. In 1939 Kuenzle took part in the Hagana's clandestine officers' course. At the outbreak of the Second World War, Kuenzle became the first Jew to volunteer for service in the British army. He served with distinction throughout the war, and quickly impressed his British commanders with his military and organizational skills. During the war, both Kuenzle's parents were murdered by the Nazis in concentration camps. In May 1948, as the newly independent State of Israel created its armed forces, Kuenzle was called up to serve as an artillery officer. He participated in heavy fighting during the War of Independence and played a major role in the creation of the IDF artillery corps. Today, a Napoleonic cannon stands in his garden – a token of appreciation from the artillery corps to the commander of its training base.

After seven years in the Israeli army, Kuenzle decided it was time to leave. He had spent a large part of his adult life in uniform and sought a quieter life with his family. However, old soldiers never retire and men of Kuenzle's experience were in short supply in Israel at that time. Kuenzle was approached by the IDF Deputy Chief of Staff, who asked him to volunteer for a secret mission involving the security of Jews living in Arab countries in North Africa.

Kuenzle could not refuse. He travelled undercover to North Africa, where he worked tirelessly for four years developing clandestine defensive capabilities for Jewish communities and facilitating secret emigration to Israel. Kuenzle became a Mossad agent and gained extensive experience operating in the secret world of espionage.

The Cukurs operation can only be fully understood within the context of the development of the Mossad and the people behind it. The Mossad evolved from the Jewish underground organizations that operated during the British Mandate period in Palestine. During the First World War, British forces captured Palestine from the Ottoman Empire. The British ruled Palestine until 1948 and prevented the free immigration of Jews into the area. The Jewish leadership in Palestine set up secret military underground organizations as a nucleus for a future Jewish army. The main group was the Hagana (Hebrew for 'defence'), which developed its own intelligence section to spy on Arab and British forces. This small intelligence section later developed into a sophisticated, information-gathering organization that recruited and ran agents all over the Middle East.[1]

The intelligence activities of the Hagana expanded during the Second World War, as thousands of young Jews enlisted into the British army to fight the Nazis. Many of those recruits originally came from Eastern European countries and could speak many European languages fluently. They were recruited by the British Special Operations Executive (SOE), trained in espionage and commando techniques and then parachuted into Nazi-occupied Europe to assist partisan and resistance groups. Many were captured and killed, but the training of those agents formed a base for enhancing the skills of a new generation of young Jewish intelligence in the Hagana. The commander of the Hagana intelligence section in Tel-Aviv was Isser Harel, a man who later shaped the Israeli intelligence community into the formidable force it is today.

Shortly after Israel's independence in May 1948, Israeli Prime Minister David Ben-Gurion appointed Isser Harel to the position of *Memune* – the official in charge of Israel's civilian intelligence services. Harel, who gained considerable operational experience in the Hagana, organized the Mossad in the form it is today and under his 12-year leadership it became a highly professional service with global capabilities.[2] He was also responsible for Israel's internal security service, the Shabak. Under Harel's leadership, the Mossad had become not only a work-place but also an extended family. It took great care of its people, the most valuable resource of any intelligence organization, according to Harel. This care also extended to the families of Mossad agents, as agents were often away from Israel for many years, unable to inform their families of their activities or whereabouts.

The formative experiences of the Mossad led to the establishment of a key principle for the Israeli intelligence community, which was to influence its work for many decades. This principle was that Israel's intelligence community is not only responsible for collecting information for the benefit of the state but also operates for the protection of Jews all over the world. In practical terms, the Jewish and Zionist character of the Israeli intelligence services meant that Mossad activities branched into areas not traditionally dealt with by intelligence services. Such tasks included assisting clandestine Jewish immigration from Arab countries and later also from the Soviet Union, the defence of Jewish communities in dangerous areas and the hunt for Nazi war criminals.[3] These tasks not only took up much of the Mossad's scant resources but also gave it direct access to top political decision-makers, who perceived the Mossad as an integral tool in the Jewish people's fight for survival. It was this role that was to take the Mossad across the world in its hunt for Nazi criminals such as Eichmann and Cukurs.

The Mossad was a small intelligence service at the time, and its first priority was the security of Israel, threatened by its Arab neighbours. Little time and effort could be spared for locating Nazi criminals, many of whom had escaped after the war to Latin America, but, in 1960, the Mossad embarked on a daring operation that would bring to trial one of the most notorious Nazi war criminals, Adolf Eichmann. An ardent Nazi, Eichmann was considered 'the architect of the Final Solution'.[4] A senior SS officer and specialist on Jewish issues,

Eichmann was responsible for the extensive transport operation that brought Jews to their final destination, the gas chambers. He played a key role in coordinating the activities of all Nazi government ministries and services for the extermination of the Jews. Even when the tide turned against Germany and the war seemed to be lost, Eichmann did his best to send as many Jews as possible to the death camps. In late 1944, as Russian tanks were rolling towards Budapest, he insisted that over 100,000 Hungarian Jews be deported to Auschwitz. Eichmann even took over trains allocated for sending Wehrmacht troops to the front and used them instead to send more Jews to their death. In August 1944 he proudly reported to Heinrich Himmler that 6 million Jews had been killed in the gas chambers and by the *Einsatzgruppen* death squads.[5] At the end of the war, Eichmann changed his identity and disappeared.[6]

In September 1957 the Mossad received information indicating the possibility that Eichmann was living with his family in Buenos Aires. A Mossad agent was dispatched to Argentina to investigate this information, but he was unable to locate Eichmann on the basis of the sketchy and incomplete information. The head of the Mossad, Isser Harel, was determined to bring Eichmann to justice in Israel. Both he and Prime Minister Ben-Gurion believed that putting Eichmann on public trial would reveal many details of the Holocaust from one of its prime instigators and would have major historical and educational value. Accordingly, the Mossad set Eichmann as a high priority for location and kidnapping.

By early 1960 the Mossad had gained enough information to conclusively identify Eichmann. In April 1960, a Mossad team was dispatched to Argentina. Operating over 8,000 miles from their base, the Mossad agents located Eichmann's house in Buenos Aires' Garibaldi Street and were able to kidnap Eichmann as he returned home from work.[7] Having admitted to being the wanted Nazi war criminal, Eichmann was held at a secret Mossad safe house until a way could be found to bring him clandestinely to Israel. Eleven days later Eichmann was smuggled on board a special El-Al flight, which came to Buenos Aires to participate in Argentina's 150th Year of Independence. He was brought to Israel and handed over to the police.

The daring kidnap of Eichmann stunned the world. The activities of a small group of agents, operating on the other side of the world without any local support, had all the suspense, action and drama of a classic spy story. Eichmann's trial was covered by hundreds of journalists and quickly became the media spectacle of the decade. But the few agents who participated in the kidnapping were not allowed to talk and kept their story secret for many years. In the absence of reliable information, newspapers printed wild stories, many of them contradictory, on how Eichmann was captured. In Israel, strict military censorship prevented the publication of the real details of the operation, fearing that the military regime in Argentina would take revenge on the Jewish population in that country. Only in 1990 was the first comprehensive and reliable account of this operation made public.[8] Eichmann was tried before a special Israeli court. In December 1961 he was found guilty and sentenced to death. He was hanged at Ramle prison in May 1962.

Unaware of Eichmann's identification in Argentina, Kuenzle met Isser Harel to report on a successful mission in a distant Asian country. Impressed with his organizational skills and ability to assume any cover identity, Harel brought Kuenzle into the Eichmann operation, where he played a key role. Following the successful conclusion of the Eichmann kidnapping, Kuenzle returned to his duties in Israel. He was later posted abroad, where he first learned about the Cukurs mission.

In 1963 Harel resigned following disagreements with Prime Minister David Ben-Gurion over the activities of German scientists working on Egypt's military rockets programme. Ben-Gurion appointed General Meir Amit head of the Mossad. Amit, an experienced military officer, had previously headed Israel's military intelligence branch, AMAN. Amit had known Kuenzle since 1948, when he commanded Israeli forces desperately trying to stop the Egyptian invasion of the Negev desert. Meir Amit brought with him a new spirit to the Mossad. With Amit at the helm, it turned into a modern organization based on structured methods and institutionalized training and development. Amit was the first to bring computers into intelligence work, as he sought to expand the Mossad's operational capabilities through modern means of management and control. Under Amit's leadership, the Mossad initiated and carried out the Cukurs operation.

One question hanging over the Cukurs mission is why Cukurs was killed and not kidnapped like Eichmann. The answer is threefold. First, the small Mossad was unable to invest such extensive resources in terms of personnel and funds into the Cukurs mission at a time when Israel was facing a potential war on three fronts. Second, the pressing time element, compounded by the imminent debate in Germany over the Statute of Limitations on Nazi war crimes, precluded the extensive operational requirements of a kidnapping operation. Finally, the nature of the Nazi criminal himself was different. Eichmann was a bureaucrat, a manager on a grand scale of the Holocaust, often described as a 'desk murderer'. He possessed unique inside knowledge on the Nazi crimes that was vital for preserving the historical legacy of the Holocaust. As such, his trial had unique historical value. Cukurs, on the other hand, was a low-level, sadistic killer, whose crimes were characterized by their brutal violence and sheer inhumanity. The horrific nature of his crimes seemed to justify a violent punishment.

Once the Uruguayan police discovered the body of Cukurs, the story made newspaper headlines all over the world. Cukurs' execution had a profound affect on Nazi criminals living in hiding all over Latin America, who were stunned to learn that the long arm of the Mossad could reach a person like Cukurs, who lived comfortably under the protection of the authorities. Many wanted Nazi criminals who had until then lived quite openly in large cities went underground and escaped to live in small, distant rural communities. Many Nazis cut off their contacts with old comrades, fearing betrayal by those who knew of their past. While many former Nazis convinced themselves after the Eichmann kidnapping that the Mossad was only after the principal Nazi leader, the Cukurs operation demonstrated that even a relatively minor Nazi criminal could be targeted.

Despite its success, the Cukurs operation was not followed by further Mossad operations against wanted Nazi war criminals. By early 1967, Israel was expecting to be attacked by its Arab neighbours on three fronts and all available intelligence resources were set towards countering this threat. The Six Day War of June 1967 and the subsequent occupation of the West Bank and the Gaza Strip brought Israeli control over 1.5 million Palestinians. In the ensuing years, terrorism became the paramount challenge facing Israeli intelligence and their scant resources could not be diverted to the Nazi issue. Efforts to discover wanted Nazis further declined after the 1973 Yom Kippur War, when the Egyptian and Syrian armies successfully mounted a surprise attack against Israel. The Arab military surprise brought Israel to the verge of defeat. Although Israeli forces were able to reverse the tide of the war and invade Arab territory, the war ended in a political stalemate. After the war, much criticism was levelled at the intelligence community for having spent much of its limited resources on matters secondary to monitoring Arab military activities. As a result, intelligence efforts were concentrated on Arab countries and terror organizations.[9]

By the 1980s, most of the wanted Nazi criminals had died in hiding and international interest in their fate declined. However, in February 1986, John Ivan Demjanjuk, a former Ukrainian who was living in the United States, was extradited to Israel to stand trial for Nazi war crimes. US authorities determined that during the Second World War, Demjanjuk had been an SS guard at the Treblinka Nazi death camp. He was accused of being responsible for the death of numerous concentration camp inmates, many of whom were put to death in the most horrifying ways. Demjanjuk's trial in Israel commenced in February 1987 under wide media interest resembling that of the Eichmann trial two decades earlier. The trial lasted over two years and included testimonies from death-camp survivors and former SS officers. Much of the trial concentrated on the issue of Demjanjuk's real identity, since he denied being the notorious camp guard christened 'Ivan the Terrible' by the camp inmates.

In April 1988, a special tribunal of the Israeli courts found Demjanjuk guilty on all counts and sentenced him to death. Demjanjuk appealed and new information over his case, made available after the collapse of the Soviet Union, was obtained from Russia. In 1993 the Israeli Supreme Court decided to acquit Demjanjuk for reasons of doubts over his identity. The Demjanjuk trial was the last such attempt in Israel to bring a Nazi criminal to justice.

In 1991, Kuenzle decided to write a book on the Cukurs operation and was able to obtain the consent of the Mossad, which is notoriously reluctant to approve former officers' memoirs. But, in this case, the Mossad leadership was convinced that the Cukurs story had a special historical importance and permitted Kuenzle to publish what had, until then, been state secrets. Kuenzle's motivation for writing the book was his deep personal commitment to legacy of the Holocaust. The memory of his parents, murdered by the Nazis in concentration camps, was indelibly imprinted in his mind. He wanted to tell a generation of young Israelis of the Mossad attempts to see that justice was done regarding a Nazi criminal such as Cukurs.

The Execution of the Hangman of Riga was first published in Hebrew in 1997 and became an instant bestseller. It was not only the first account of the Cukurs operation, hitherto known only to a few intelligence insiders, but was also the first account of such a mission by its principal organizer. The book sheds new light on Mossad tradecraft and on the way the Nazi issue was perceived inside the organization. In 2002, Frank Cass of London decided to publish this first edition of the manuscript in English.

Following the Cukurs operation, Kuenzle returned to his duties at the Mossad, where he served until his retirement in 1981. He had successfully used many dozens of different identities throughout his career without ever being caught, well illustrating his unique capacity to blend into any surrounding. Even today, Kuenzle continues to use his exceptional experience for the benefit of new generations of intelligence officers in Israel.

Other members of the Cukurs operation continued their intelligence careers. Yoav, born in 1923 in Haifa and a former member of the 'Palmach', was a battalion commander during Israel's 1948 War of Independence. In 1956 he joined the

Israeli military intelligence (AMAN), where he commanded the Operations Unit. When the head of AMAN, General Mei Amit, was appointed head of the Mossad in 1963 he brought with him Yoav and his unit. Yoav proved to be a dedicated and talented commander in covert operations. He died in 1998. Dova'le, who came to the Mossad after distinguished service in the famous 'Unit 101' commando, was killed by enemy fire on the Egyptian front during the October 1973 Yom Kippur War. Oswald Taussig, who joined the Mossad in the early 1950s, was known throughout his intelligence career as a person who could establish contacts everywhere and with everyone. Retired, he now lives in Israel, as does Arie, who originally came to the Mossad as part of Yoav's military intelligence unit.

Anton Kuenzle is living in Israel, the country to which he dedicated his life. Having recently celebrated Israel's 55th Independence Day, Kuenzle is aware, perhaps more than most other people, how fragile and precarious Israel's security was in its early years. The example set by Kuenzle and his fellow agents inspires Israel's young generation of intelligence officers. The story of the execution of the Hangman of Riga became a legend within the intelligence community and is taught at its intelligence school. It is the story of one man against a vicious Nazi, of one Israeli sent to enact justice on a Nazi war criminal who had set out to destroy Jewish people. The lessons of the Cukurs operation are still as relevant today as they were when Herbert Cukurs paid the ultimate price for his murderous crimes.

Shlomo Shpiro
Jerusalem, May 2003

NOTES

1. For the history and development of the Hagana intelligence section see E. Dekel, *The Story of Shay*, Tel-Aviv, 1959.
2. For Harel's biography and career see M. Bar Zohar, *Spies in the Promised Land: Isser Harel and the Israeli Secret*

Service, London, 1972.

3. For the Zionist tasks of the Mossad see Yossi Melman and Dan Raviv, *Every Spy a Prince*, Boston, MA, 1990.
4. For Eichmann's work against the Jews see Stanley Blumberg and Gwinn Owens, *The Survival Factor: Israeli Intelligence from WWI to the Present*, New York, 1981, pp. 17–19, 64–71.
5. Louis Snyder, *Encyclopedia of the Third Reich*, Ware, 1998, pp. 80–1.
6. Before Eichmann's kidnapping, many accounts were published in the press about his alleged wealth and travels to Arab countries. Some even claimed that 'he had at his disposal no fewer than seventy passports'. However, those were mostly Mossad disinformation exercises intended to make Eichmann believe his trail was lost. See, for example, R. Deacon, *The Israeli Secret Service*, London, 1977, pp. 103–6.
7. For details on the kidnapping see Zvi Malhin and Uri Dan, *Eichmann is in my Hand*, Tel-Aviv, 1987.
8. See Isser Harel, *The House on Garibaldi Street*, edited by Shlomo Shpiro, London, 1997.
9. For the Mossad operations after the Cukurs mission see Ian Black and Benny Morris, *Israel's Secret Wars*, New York, 1991.
10. Former intelligence officers in Israel are obliged to obtain the approval of their old service and that of the Israeli military censorship for any manuscript they wish to publish.

1
DEATH BEARS GREETINGS

THE ELDERLY pilot held with steady hands the control stick of the small aircraft that was circling a few hundred yards above the vast city of São Paulo. The city of millions was visible through the haze, sprawling all the way to the horizon, from the slums on the outskirts to the skyscrapers in the heart of this business and industrial centre of Brazil. Endless columns of cars, which looked from above like diligently marching ants or beetles – the most popular car in Brazil at the time – continued to head on that Saturday, 19 September 1964, toward the recreation resorts the city dwellers favoured on weekends.

'I love the view from up here. Pretty sight, isn't it?' said the pilot. A well-worn overall which had seen better days covered his muscular body. His large ears supported thickly framed glasses, which had been broken and mended haphazardly with a piece of aluminium wire. The lenses were rather thick, and resembled the bottom of milk bottles, but nothing stood in his way of piloting the light airplane with great dexterity. His slight, almost automatic movements attested to his wealth of aviation experience, which compensated for the eyesight that had been gradually failing over the years.

'In just a few minutes, Herr Kuenzle, we shall return and land on the lake,' he continued in his fluent German with just a trace of foreign accent, and motioned to the large water reservoir below that glittered in the sun. 'You can see my marina from here,' he shouted, trying to overcome the noise of the engine. There was pride in his voice when he said 'my marina'.

He took a gentle, almost imperceptible turn to the right in order to allow Anton Kuenzle, the Austrian businessman who had hired his services for the short flight over São Paulo, fully to appreciate the view. The pilot used this simple manoeuvre to throw another glance at his passenger. He saw a medium-built man, slightly balding, wearing glasses, with a dark thick moustache that barely covered two large moles. He estimated his passenger's age at 45, give or take.

The passenger, clad in elegant yet casual clothes, did not say much during the 20-minute flight in the small seaplane. He just listened attentively to the pilot's descriptions of the sights below. Kuenzle knew exactly what they were circling, even without the explanations of the pilot, who had introduced himself before boarding the plane as Herbert Cukurs.

Without difficulty he located the orange VW Beetle with which he had arrived at Cukurs' small marina on the shore of the Represa do Guarapiranga, the western part of São Paulo's artificial water reservoir. The long beaches of the lake served as popular bathing and recreation sites. His Beetle was parked next to the thatched country restaurant, where he had had a sumptuous lunch before walking down to the shore. He had wished to inform himself about the scope of the tourist business in this region.

The flight over São Paulo passed quickly.

'Thank you, Herr Cukurs. That was a very pleasant flight,' said Kuenzle once the pilot killed the engine following their smooth landing on the water and the careful navigation of the plane through the dozens of row and pedal boats of the weekend vacationers all the way back to its anchorage. Kuenzle's German was perfect, flawless. It bore no trace of dialect, and was in fact classical German. His whole manner of speech attested to the fact that he was a well-educated man.

Cukurs closely examined his passenger one more time. He somehow had the feeling that he and Kuenzle had more in common than just the tourist trade. 'It would give me pleasure if you would join me for a toast on my boat,' Cukurs invited his client cordially. 'On the water I could answer all your questions on tourism in the São Paulo area in peace.'

Kuenzle glanced at his watch in the typical fashion of business people, who somehow always look as if they are about to miss a very important appointment. He weighed up whether he should accept the unexpected offer. 'Gladly, Herr Cukurs. With pleasure,' he finally said, taking extra caution to conceal how glad he really was over the old pilot's invitation; the old pilot who ran a not-too-prosperous boat-rental business, and who arranged the occasional flight for well-off tourists.

In the small cabin of his motorboat, Cukurs produced a bottle of local brandy and two glasses. 'Prost,' he toasted his new acquaintance.

'Prost,' responded Kuenzle, as he raised the glass with his right hand. His toast sounded genuine and sincere to Cukurs, a heartfelt good wish. Cukurs could not have been more wrong. He could not have known that Kuenzle's good wishes were meant to send him in one direction only – to Cukurs' own grave.

The name of the pleasant well-wisher was not Kuenzle, and he was no Austrian businessman. He was in fact Israeli, a veteran high-ranking officer in the Israel Defence Forces, and a senior agent with the Mossad (Israel's CIA equivalent). He had come to Brazil with only one purpose in mind: to locate the Hangman of Riga, who, during the Second World War, had been personally responsible for the annihilation of tens of thousands of Riga's Jews. His goal was to win the Hangman's confidence and trust, then lure him into the trap where he would be sentenced to death and executed by 'those who shall never forget'.

The Hangman of Riga, the criminal who brought death and suffering upon the Jews of Latvia, was none other than Herbert Cukurs.

2
THE MISSION

ALTHOUGH THE first autumn leaves fell on the pavements, the faces of the Parisians stuck in the proverbial traffic jam still glowed with the dark suntans of their summer vacation, their sacred *vacances.*

'Twenty-Five Years Ago Today Sounded The First Shots Of The Second World War', I read in passing the screaming newspaper headlines on the counter of the corner kiosk. The newspapers recruited this historical date for their circulation wars, and the readers interpreted the significance of the occasion, which had started with the Nazi invasion of Poland, according to their individual political leanings.

How time flies. The thought crossed my mind as I made my way to the meeting Yoav had called for the morning hours of this day, 1 September 1964. The meeting was to take place in a modest rented apartment in one of the apartment blocks on the Avenue de Versailles, not far from the banks of the Seine.

I crossed the Pont de Grenelle, with the small Statue of Liberty at its foot. Except for its proportions, it was identical to the Statue of Liberty that watches over the gateway to New York. Walking at the slow pace of a tourist who has all the time in the world, I passed by the singular structure of Radio France, making sure that I arrived alone, without any superfluous tails such as a stalking unit of one of the many intelligence services that were somewhat hyperactive in Paris in those days.

It's hard to believe that 25 years have already passed since then, I thought. Yet I remembered everything so vividly, as if it had happened only yesterday. The bitter arguments among the students of the Haifa Technological Institute in those fateful days when the war broke out in far-off Europe, where many of us still had families. The nostalgic recollections brought a smile to my face. Most of my friends then had volunteered for the local defence force, but I had decided to go all the way. I did not believe that by standing guard for hours on end on top of one of the watch towers of the internment camps the British had established for the German Templers in Sharona or Waldheim would contribute anything to the victory over the Nazi beast. I had had personal experience of living in Germany under Nazi rule. I wanted to make a real contribution to the defeat of the Nazis, and so I enlisted in the Royal Artillery. I was the first Jew in Palestine to enlist in the British army, long before the Jewish community's national institutions called upon the youth to enlist. It had already been said of me that I was a misfit, an individualist who always chose his own path.

'Bonjour!' I smiled at the concierge who scrutinized everyone who entered or left the building through the small window of her apartment. What a great invention, the concierge, I thought. At least from the point of view of the security services. Nothing escapes the beady, watchful eyes of these old hags.

I stopped my musings when I pressed the bell to the door behind which our meeting was to take place.

'Hi, Yitzhak, I'm glad you made it,' said Yoav, who had called the meeting. He opened the door only after peeking through the peephole and making sure I was not an uninvited guest.

'From this moment onwards your name is Anton Kuenzle. You'd better start getting used to it.'

I had no idea what he was talking about, and with a questioning heart entered the small guestroom, where Michael, an old friend, was already waiting.

'You must be wondering why I summoned you here, and in such a hurry,' said Yoav, opening our makeshift meeting that took place around a small coffee table. 'Well, it all begins with the final confirmation we received about a Nazi war criminal who lives in one of the South American countries under his real name, together with his family, and under the protection of the security services of that country.'

Michael and I exchanged glances that said we had known all along the reason for this meeting: Nazis.

Yoav, a former member of the Palmach, the pre-state illegal paramilitary organization, who stayed in uniform after the establishment of Israel, rose to a high rank in the Israel Defence Forces and then went on to serve in the Mossad, Israel's CIA, was a well-built, suntanned man in his forties, with a shock of hair that was rather silvery for his age. He proceeded with his explanations.

'In a few months, on 8 May 1965 to be precise, the world will mark 20 years since the victory over Nazi Germany, which annihilated most of the Jews in Europe. There are already voices, and not in Germany alone, which say that it is time to look forward, to draw a line under the events of the past, to erase the memories of all the horrors, to forget the Nazis, and to apply the Statute of Limitations to their crimes.

'As you know, Western Europe is undergoing a process of unification, which may bring about the elimination of all borders there. West Germany plays a central role in this process,' he continued in a quiet, measured voice. 'A fierce public debate regarding this issue is raging in Germany, but not only there. The German elite is filled with people from all walks of life who would prefer to erase from their curriculum vitae the answer to "Where were you and what did you do in the years between 1933 to 1945?" The supporters of the implementation of the Statute of Limitations have plenty of arguments for why legal proceedings against the Nazis should be halted. They find it convenient, for instance, to use a formal argument, namely that the Statute of Limitations, which was enacted as a law in Germany in 1871, should apply not only to ordinary murders and crimes; it should also apply to such crimes as genocide and the Nazi horrors. Let me just point out the German Minister of Justice, Ewald Bucher, who was, according to our information, a card-holding member of the Nazi party at the time. Of course he supports the implementation of the Statute of Limitations. According to him, most "great" Nazis have already been apprehended and put on trial, and thus the whole matter can be closed down quietly . . .

'Since the end of the war, 61,000 Nazi criminals have stood trial in Germany. But only 6,100 were convicted. There are an additional 13,000 cases in various stages, from preliminary investigation to the completion of court proceedings. If the Statute of Limitations is implemented, all these cases will be closed.'

Yoav took a break to sip from his coffee which had turned cold while he was speaking. We listened to his words with keen interest.

'Politicians follow public opinion closely, and they report that an overwhelming majority of German citizens wish to draw a line under their Nazi past. They don't want to deal with Nazis anymore. What interests them now is the sweet life of the "economic miracle" era. But the politicians, unlike the citizens, must also take into account the international sensitivity regarding this issue. For instance, the heavy pressure exerted on the Bonn government by Jewish organizations in the United States. This is why the politicians are now scrabbling around for solutions.

'In Bonn, the West German capital, they are debating a proposal to extend the Statute of Limitations for another ten years, which means until 1975. But the chances of accepting this proposal are small, mostly due to constitutional and legal difficulties.

'Another proposal has been initiated by the father of the Federal Republic of Germany, Dr Konrad Adenauer. It suggests that the Statute of Limitations should be counted from 1949 and not 1945, since the Federal Republic was established in 1949, and only then began the systematic process of putting Nazi war criminals on trial. This proposal has some chance of being accepted as a compromise solution, and therein lies its danger. All it really means is that the criminals who have not been apprehended yet will only be able to crawl out of their hiding holes in September 1969, rather than in 1965.

'But as you may have gathered by yourselves, according to German public opinion polls there is no guarantee that the politicians are prepared to extend the Statute of Limitations, not by four years, not by ten years, and, for that matter, most probably not at all.

'But those who have a vested interest in forgetting the past and in implementing the Statute of Limitations on Nazi war crimes can be found not only in Germany. Anyone who carefully scrutinizes the past of some top European leaders may run into some embarrassing details connected to the Nazi era. A French newspaper recently published an article exposing a dark corner in the biography of François Mitterrand during the Vichy regime. Mitterrand is one of the Socialist leaders who has his eyes set on the Elysée Palace, the official residence of the President of France. And he is not the only one around with dark corners in his past. This may explain why the idea of applying the Statute of Limitations to Nazi war crimes has so many supporters from across the political spectrum.

'It's true that it's been only four years since Israeli Mossad agents kidnapped Adolf Eichmann from Argentina and brought him to stand trial in a court of law in Jerusalem. The affair raised public consciousness throughout the world of the Nazi horrors, but it seems that the strong impact of the Eichmann kidnapping and of the horrifying testimonies that were given in his trial is losing its effect.

'We, Israelis and Jews, have the obligation to stop this sweeping trend,' Yoav declared. Outwardly he stayed calm, but it was impossible to overlook the rising intensity in his voice as he continued speaking.

'It is absolutely inconceivable that tens of thousands of Nazi war criminals who never paid for their heinous crimes should now be able to crawl out of their hiding holes and spend the rest of their lives in peace and tranquillity, secure and immune from investigations and arrests. This is nothing but a sweeping reprieve!' His voice rose. 'It's been only 20 years since the release of the survivors of the death camps, and we owe it to them, and to the 6 million who did not survive and are unable to avenge themselves – we must thwart this shameful process of the Statute of Limitations.'

Michael and I had plenty of experience in clandestine operations in foreign countries, and right from Yoav's opening words, we had a good idea of where it was leading. We were not wrong.

'If we succeed in the operation we are now preparing, we'll once again put the fear of death into the hearts of tens of thousands Nazi war criminals. We'll do everything in our capacity to make the rest of their lives miserable. They will fear their own shadow. They will not dare to leave their homes, and will have continuous nightmares of anonymous assassins, the offspring of their innocent victims, seeking their revenge. They must not have one single moment of peace and tranquillity until their last dying day on earth!' Yoav paused briefly to clear his throat.

'Our friend Dova'le went to South America to check on some information we received. The data we have gathered indicate that one of the worst and most sadistic criminals lives securely in Brazil. We are not dealing here with a desk murderer like Eichmann, who only followed orders and constructed a death machine that operated with satanic efficiency; someone who took care of everything, from the technical coordination with the Reich's railway services to the ordering of the Zyklon B gas at the IG Farben factories. No, the Nazi I am speaking of is a completely different type from Eichmann. He, with his own hands, smashed the heads of babies, shot old people and tortured women. But he managed to escape punishment, and he is waiting, like thousands of other Nazi war criminals, for that moment when society will allow them to return and become part of it again, as if all the horrors they committed had never happened. But we have decided not to let that happen. We have decided to see to it that he receives the punishment he deserves. And we'll make sure that his execution, as well as the record of his past crimes, will make the headlines of every newspaper in the world. This will not only instill fear in the escaped criminals in hiding but, more importantly, it will sway public opinion to strongly oppose this deplorable idea of applying the Statute of Limitations to Nazi war crimes.' Yoav paused again and sipped from the cold coffee before announcing, 'The Nazi whose turn has come is Herbert Cukurs.'

I ran the name through my mind, to no avail. As if reading my thoughts, Yoav proceeded to explain.

'Cukurs was a Latvian Nazi who surpassed his "spiritual" mentors in his cruelty. He is personally accountable for the annihilation of at least 30,000 Jews in Riga, and was awarded the titles of the "Hangman of Riga" and the "Butcher of Riga", and with very good reason. I have here some survivors' testimonies of Cukurs' crimes during the war.' He pointed to a fairly thin file on the coffee table. 'It's just inconceivable. We are dealing here with a despicable sadist who actually enjoyed torturing his victims and murdering innocent people. And this Cukurs has the *chutzpah* to give interviews to Brazilian newspapers, and claim that he is innocent, that he has no idea what anyone would want with him. He doesn't even shy away from complaining about being persecuted. And after telling everyone about his innocence, he parades his SS uniform with great pride before the cameras.'

Yoav looked directly at me.

'I propose that you, Yitzhak, go to Brazil disguised as an Austrian businessman under the name of Anton Kuenzle,' Yoav continued with the briefing. 'First you'll have to build yourself a suitable cover story that will allow you to travel freely in South America. Your mission, Yitzhak, provided you volunteer for it of course, is to establish contact with Cukurs, gain his confidence and befriend him. You have operational experience, the right qualifications, the looks, and a great talent for languages. I have full confidence that you will succeed in carrying out this difficult mission.'

Outwardly I kept a poker face. But I felt my heart race and my adrenaline level skyrocket suddenly. So many different thoughts ran through my mind. I released a deep breath. Having been born in Germany and having lost both parents in the Holocaust, I needed no lengthy detailed explanations of that terrible era. My father, a well-known doctor in our hometown, served during the First World War as a medical officer in the Prussian army and for his service in the cruel battles of Mars-la-Tour on the western front was awarded the Iron Cross. This fact did not stop the Nazis from sending him to his death in the Theresienstadt concentration camp. My mother was deported to Auschwitz, where she was murdered as part of what the Nazis and their abettors termed 'the final solution to the Jewish problem'.

To my regret, the State of Israel did not carry out many operations against Nazis, mainly because the young state faced real existential problems. Its intelligence services could not afford to deal with settling the historical account with the Nazis. There were enough immediate problems that threatened the future of the state, and kept its security services fully occupied. The result was that the little Nazi-hunting that was done was a concentrated effort to locate those criminals who topped the wanted list: Eichmann, Mengele, Bormann and 'Gestapo Müller'. I heard the name Cukurs, though, for the first time in my life in this small apartment in the 16th arrondissement in Paris.

'I'm well aware that this is no simple task,' Yoav continued, addressing me. 'This complicated operation demands that you go to a distant country, where you will face a criminal who is, according to our reports, cunning, mistrustful, ruthless and dangerous, and is always prepared for the worst. We know that he resides in a well-protected home, almost a fortress, surrounded by barbed-wire fences and guard dogs.'

I did not react.

'We're actually asking the impossible of you – to penetrate Cukurs' wall of mistrust to the point that he trusts you enough to leave Brazil. He's been living there since 1960 under the protection of the local security service. You may well ask why is it so important to get him out of Brazil in order to execute him. The answer is not simple. First, we must protect the Jews of Brazil from any possible reprisals by Nazis and other anti-Semites. In addition, lest we forget, the death penalty has not yet been abolished in Brazil, and if something in this operation goes awry and one of us is caught and apprehended, God forbid, the whole thing could end up badly... So it's preferable to carry out our operation in a more liberal country, where the police force is more observant of prisoners' rights. For example, Uruguay.'

This last comment somehow broke the tension in the air. Michael started leafing through the documents Yoav had brought.

'It says here that this Cukurs lives in São Paulo, in a neighbourhood called Interlagos, on the shores of some artificial lake. It appears that he runs a small boat-rental business and even offers seaplane sightseeing flights,' he said. Then, after a short pause he asked, 'Will Yitzhak actually operate alone, or will we send a small stalking and protection unit with him?'

'I prefer to work alone,' I interjected quickly, before anyone present had a chance to form an opinion on the matter. 'I'd rather work without tails or protection. My gut feeling tells me that such an operation can be carried out only alone. A lone wolf. Me against the target. One on one. Without any background activities that could only complicate the situation and endanger the entire mission.'

Yoav nodded. My outburst was in fact a declaration that I volunteered for the mission. The idea of sending me to Brazil as Anton Kuenzle was confirmation of my friends' high regard for my qualifications as a field operator.

I had behind me many years of operational experience throughout the world. Along the way I had acquired quite a few talents, particularly the reputation of someone who becomes totally immersed in the fictional character of any operational cover story. In my daily life, I was a quiet, introverted man, not particularly pushy or demanding. But also a man of principles, who could be as stubborn as a mule when it came to the things that really mattered. The minute I undertook a mission, I would undergo an amazing transformation. I would become a different person, someone with an ordinary face that attracted no attention, who could disappear in any crowd without an effort. I felt confident, even assertive, and had the capacity to strike up conversations and gain the trust of the people I met. All this made me a natural candidate for the main role in Operation Cukurs.

'All right,' Yoav consented. 'Yitzhak, Anton will operate alone. I trust him 100 per cent. Now it's only a question of time before we settle the account with Cukurs. We should actually give this Cukurs a new name from now on. I think we'll call him "The Deceased". But we must get down to brass tacks – we must learn who this Cukurs is, and how we can best help Yitzhak quickly assume the identity of the Austrian businessman, Anton Kuenzle.'

3
YITZHAK BECOMES ANTON

THE TRANS-EUROPE Express that left the Gare du Nord in Paris in the early hours of the morning rolled slowly into Rotterdam's main train station. On the outskirts of the town loomed a forest of the harbour's tall cranes. It was one of Europe's largest and busiest ports, with hundreds of ships anchoring there daily. The town swarmed with busy people, local and foreign – from sailors on brief leave to business people of varying degrees of respectability. In short, Rotterdam was a very convenient place for creating a suitable cover story.

Three days had passed since the meeting with Yoav and Michael in the small rented apartment in Paris. My mission was clear – to go to South America, locate Cukurs, gain his confidence and trust, and prepare the ground for his execution. No one was standing over me with a stopwatch, measuring how long it would take me to create a cover story that would allow me to operate freely in Brazil as Anton Kuenzle, but I had decided to move fast and conclude this stage, so vital for carrying out the operation, as speedily as possible. I felt I had no time to lose.

I had used the long hours in which the train crossed the monotonous terrain of northern France, Belgium and Holland to prepare my next moves. I had left Paris on Friday morning in order to reach Rotterdam at midday, which would leave me almost five hours to conduct my business. The following day, Saturday, most of the businesses and offices would only be open for half a day, giving me an additional five hours. In total, nearly ten hours in this town in order to create a cover story for an operation in a distant country. Despite the long list of chores and the short time, I felt I had a good chance of completing them.

Rotterdam was not utterly foreign to me, and I knew that all the official offices and businesses that I would need were situated downtown, in a radius of several hundred metres around the main train station.

Once off the train, I called the Hilton Hotel. 'Sorry, sir. All the rooms are occupied. I don't have a single room available,' said the reservations clerk. I should have thought about it earlier and booked a room from Paris. Still, it was not the end of the world. I had thought of the Hilton as it could have served as a respectable address, but a large town like Rotterdam offered many other possibilities. Another phone call booked me a room in another luxury hotel, the Rijnhotel, which although not part of a prestigious international hotel chain, was well known to everyone in Rotterdam. It was exactly what I needed.

As the hotel was in Schouwburgplein, a mere few minutes away from the train station, I walked there quickly, taking in the pleasant autumn sun. Downtown was packed with traffic, and I was glad to see that the industrious Dutch people had managed to rebuild their town, which had been so badly damaged by the heavy bombardment of the German Luftwaffe in 1940. I could not help but think of the Germans, the ones who 25 years earlier had started the cruellest war in the annals of mankind, and yet attempted time and again to arouse the world's compassion with descriptions of the horrible suffering they had endured during the war. They never tired of mentioning the destruction of Dresden or other German towns that had been razed to the ground in bombardments by American and British warplanes. Yet, as they wept bitterly over their lot, the Germans somehow always seemed to forget that it had been their own Luftwaffe planes that had first attacked major cities – Warsaw, Rotterdam, Coventry and London, to name but a few.

The thousands of people running around taking care of their various businesses were the most suitable surroundings for my own business, which was to create the identity of an Austrian businessman who had never been, and whose life span was meant to last but a few months.

Registration at the hotel was brief and efficient. The combination of my advanced baldness, round stomach, and calm appearance gave every character I had adopted in past operations the semblance of trustworthiness, which was why I had never run into difficulties in carrying out such missions. I ran up to my room, left my small suitcase on the bed, and headed for my next goal – the nearest post office.

It was a large and functional grey structure. I could only imagine the number of daily curses hurled by the hundreds of Dutch people who worked within its walls against the architect who had designed this ugly and depressing building. Yet the clerk who attended to me was delightfully charming. He may have been new at his job, as yet unspoiled, or perhaps he belonged to that rare breed of polite and courteous clerks who maintain their humaneness and pleasant traits under all circumstances, and even in such a building.

'I wish to open a PO box here,' I told the clerk. There was nothing unusual about my request. Such requests were made almost daily by the Dutch and foreign business people who had dealings with the port or its related establishments. The clerk studied my Austrian passport, issued to one Anton Kuenzle, and on the request form wrote down my temporary address in Holland – Rijnhotel, Schouwburgplein, where I had left my suitcase only a few minutes earlier.

'The box is at your disposal, sir,' said the clerk, and handed me two keys. I made the first tick on my long list of chores.

I looked at my watch and noted with satisfaction that everything was going well so far. Now all I had to do was find an open bank. Back on the main street, Coolsingel Street, I discovered a large branch of the AMRO Bank, one of the better-known financial institutions in Holland, where I encountered once again a courteous and efficient clerk. I assumed he spoke German, a language most Dutch people possess to some degree. But in the 1960s the memory of the Nazi occupation was still deeply embedded in the minds of the Dutch people, and that was why I chose to speak English with him.

'Of course, sir. With pleasure,' he said in response to my question of whether I could open a current account in this respectable establishment. The bunch of dollar notes I pulled out of my bag helped him with the reply.

'Sir, you are depositing here US$3,000,' stated the clerk after having quickly and nimbly counted the money. 'I need your address in Holland, sir.'

I gave him my PO box number, and presented the contract I had received only a few minutes earlier, which confirmed that I was the legitimate owner of a PO box in the central branch of the Royal Dutch Post in this large port town. This fact, together with my passport and respectable and serious appearance, which epitomized the 'businessman', seemed to satisfy all the bureaucratic requirements he could think of.

'Of course you are aware sir, that payment by cheque is not all that acceptable here,' the clerk volunteered. 'In Holland, the usual form of payment is bank transfers. We shall send the appropriate forms to your address today, sir. They'll be in your box by tomorrow.'

I checked my watch again. All in all I was pleased. It hadn't yet been two whole hours since the non-existent Anton Kuenzle had arrived in Rotterdam, and the Austrian businessman was already coming to life. I had an address, a PO box and a bank account. Not bad at all, I thought. Not bad for a start.

I continued with my walk, this time to the Hilton Hotel. According to the plan I was supposed to return to Rotterdam the following week in order to complete the cover story, and then I wanted to stay at the Hilton. Once my reservation was made, I said goodbye to the reservations manager and, grinning, walked toward the doorman. I reckoned that like all his colleagues in big hotels in major cities, he too served as a walking encyclopedia regarding everything that took place in the city. It was safe to assume, therefore, that he could be of assistance to me in carrying out the next stage swiftly and smoothly.

The doorman, clad in the uniform of a general from some Austro-Hungarian operetta, watched me emerge from the hotel lobby, and assumed I was a guest there. I asked him whether he knew what the procedure was for obtaining a visitor's visa to Brazil. Mass tourism was still unknown in the mid-1960s, and a trip to Brazil required special and quite complicated arrangements, complete with forms and other bureaucratic matters.

Of course he knew.

'Not that complicated, sir. Just a matter of a few relatively simple steps. Believe you me, there are some countries which are much more difficult to enter than Brazil,' said the doorman. 'A matter of completing a few forms, and submitting to a medical examination. That's all.'

Before I could ask another question, he already offered, 'If you wish, sir, I could send someone to get you the forms.'

The fat tip I pressed in his hand concluded our deal.

One of the bellboys was sent in great haste to the Brazilian Consulate. I went back inside, and spent half an hour at the bar, sipping coffee and reading a newspaper. The bellboy returned with the appropriate forms, which even included an instruction sheet in English.

My new friend the doorman, who with the sharp sense of experience marked me as a potential source of income, continued to prove his worthiness. He called a local doctor who worked with the Brazilian Consulate, made me an appointment, and summoned a taxi to take me to the clinic.

The medical was relatively superficial, and consisted mostly of a basic question and answer session. In fact, it was so insignificant that one had to wonder why it was necessary at all. The medical examination required of all those who wished to visit Brazil seemed less concerned with the prevention of the spread of disease in the country and more with the bank account of the Brazilian Consul, who no doubt had a share in the examining doctor's fees.

I emerged from the clinic equipped with an official certificate filled with stamps of every possible shape and form, which testified to the fact that I was in good health, and with an international vaccination card, that well-known yellow booklet. In the taxi on the way back downtown, I leafed through the visa forms, and discovered that the Brazilian authorities demanded I attach three passport photographs to it.

Well, Yitzhak, I said to myself, it's time to change appearances. Anton Kuenzle must not resemble you too much. We are dealing here with photographs that would sooner or later end up in the police archives, and if the operation is successful, it will only be a matter of time before someone puts two and two together and pulls out these pictures.

The fact is that following our meeting in Paris on Monday, as I had begun to make my plans, I had already started taking steps to alter my facial features. I happen to belong to the breed of men who grow a dark five o'clock shadow, and it was just a matter of days before a moustache appeared under my nose. Thus, since Tuesday, my upper lip had received a temporary reprieve from the razor blade.

But a moustache alone, thick as it may be, does not yet make the Israeli Yitzhak into the Austrian businessman Anton Kuenzle. So I decided to add heavily rimmed glasses, which together with the moustache could work miracles in altering discernible facial features. I could have used non-prescription glasses, the kind used by actors, but security considerations dictated otherwise. I knew Cukurs was mistrustful and fearful of traps, and the possibility existed, remote as it may have been, that he would find some excuse to check my glasses. Sharp-eyed observers can detect non-prescription glasses by the fact that the objects seen through them remain unaltered, and all I needed was for the operation to fail over such a trivial matter.

I found an optician on the main street, not far from the Rijnhotel. 'I'm afraid my eyesight has deteriorated lately,' I told the ophthalmologist, who lost no time in presenting me with the familiar table of ever-diminishing letters and numbers.

'I'm sorry. I don't seem to be able to read the bottom line,' I lied, and the doctor nodded his head sympathetically. After all, it was only natural that the eyesight of a man in his late forties would begin to fail. He performed a few more tests, in which I also failed to read the small letters and numbers, then made the appropriate diagnosis, wrote a prescription, and directed me to a nearby optometrist.

Everything went smoothly and efficiently there. I was shown a variety of frames, and chose ones that looked respectable and suited a serious businessman. The optometrist promised to have my glasses ready the next morning. I returned to the main street to continue with my acquisition spree. At a small print shop I ordered writing paper in various sizes, envelopes and business cards, all with the following information on them:

> Anton Kuenzle
> Managing Director – Investments
> P.O. Box 1208
> Rotterdam, Holland

'I would like to proofread the typesetting tomorrow morning,' I told the printer. The handsome advance I had paid, as well as the industriousness of the Dutch people, guaranteed that the stationary would be ready on time.

The day was coming to an end, as was my list of chores for that day. 'Clothes maketh the man' goes the old saying, and particularly in a profession like mine. It was a few minutes before closing time, but I still managed to enter one of the large clothing stores. My previous inquiries had taught me that Brazilian businessmen wear elegant black suits made of light material in the summer. Although Europe was preparing itself for winter, in the southern hemisphere September marked the beginning of spring, and I knew that I would have to spend a few weeks there. I ordered such a suit, and a few matching shirts. The tailor asked me to come in the next day for another fitting, and gave me his word of honour that the suit would be ready by the following week.

That was it for the day, I decided, having looked at the list I kept in my pocket, which was now full of ticks, one against each item.

'Quite impressive,' commented Adi, my old friend, whom I met that evening in the lobby of the Hilton. I had just run through the list of my activities for the day. I also told him that I had been collecting all sorts of receipts and notes that attested to the fact that their bearer was a resident of Rotterdam, such as a laundry receipt and a bus stub, and placed them in my wallet, as if they had been forgotten there. I had also acquired a few personal items, such as toothpaste with the price tag of a local drugstore, and a

Dutch-made soap, just in case the suspicious Cukurs decided to go through my belongings. He would find plenty of evidence to corroborate my story.

'By tomorrow, I'll have completed the first stage,' I promised Adi, who then went to report on our progress.

The next day, Saturday, 5 September 1964, ran very much like the previous day. The AMRO Bank forms waited for me, as promised, in my post office box. The typesetting at the printer's was ready for my final proofreading and authorization. I then went to the tailor for my fitting, and finally to the optometrist where the glasses lay waiting in their case, along with a receipt. I complimented the optometrist on his work, although the glasses did little to improve my eyesight. The very opposite was true. They may have even worsened my eyesight, and hastened by a few years the time when I needed real glasses. Who knows, I might have sacrificed the quality of my eyesight for the sake of settling the account with that despicable murderer, and I don't regret it for one second.

My uncompromising perfectionism, even at the cost of my own health, or my eyesight in this case, is part of my nature. When creating a cover story, I always paid close attention to all the small details, and never looked for shortcuts. When it came to such matters, I was an unrepentant pedant. I had seen too many foul-ups in my life that were the result of half-hearted preparations due to negligence or laziness. I could not allow such foul-ups in my cover stories.

At a nearby travel agent I booked a flight ticket for Paris–Rio de Janeiro–São Paulo–Montevideo–Paris for 11 September, which I paid for with one of the AMRO Bank money transfer forms.

A little over 24 hours since I had set foot in Rotterdam, I was sitting once more in the first-class compartment of the express train, this time heading in the opposite direction, back to Paris. I was exhausted, yet elated. In my relatively few hours in Rotterdam I had succeeded in transforming the Austrian businessman Anton Kuenzle from just a name in a passport into a respectable businessman, with a proper address, a current, active bank account, and a few other necessary items. This called for a small celebration, and I went to the dining car and ordered a sumptuous dinner. I remember to this day how good it tasted, definitely an exception to the commonly low gastronomic offerings of the Trans-Europe Express dining cars. A good omen, I remarked to myself as I finished my dessert.

The next day I met with Yoav and Michael in the small apartment on the Avenue de Versailles. I informed them of my accomplishments in Rotterdam, and we discussed our next moves.

'You're taking a camera with you, aren't you?' asked Yoav.

'Absolutely not!' I said. 'From what we know, Cukurs is a suspicious man. He may wonder why all of a sudden I pop up in his life, camera dangling from my shoulder. I'm supposed to be a businessman in search of profitable business opportunities in Brazil, not some tourist coming to take photographs of the Copacabana or Rio's Sugar Loaf Mountain. A camera will only raise Cukurs' suspicions. No camera. But there is another matter we must decide on. I must have some secure means by which to report to you. This is a long operation in which I fly solo. Every day I shall accumulate lots of details about Cukurs, and plenty of technical information vital for the operation's success, and I don't want to take the risk of writing down notes. I'd rather send you my reports in invisible ink every few days. I also want you to send me your instructions in invisible ink, camouflaged as innocent letters and sent to the American Express branches in São Paulo and other cities I shall reach.'

Yoav and Michael weighed up my proposal. It wasn't unreasonable, they agreed, and after a brief consultation accepted it.

'Tomorrow I'm leaving for Switzerland, to arrange the financial side,' I said as I ran my finger over my upper lip, where the first traces of an impressive moustache were already visible. 'You know, the usual – depositing money and getting letters of credit for South America.'

We then went on to discuss various ideas that would ensure the elimination of 'The Deceased', provided, of course, that I succeeded in gaining his trust, and in luring him into the death trap we were laying for him.

'This is a tight schedule. You have less than a week to complete all your preparations,' Yoav said, summing up the meeting. 'Let it be with luck, and most importantly, you take care of yourself!'

On the whole I am a level-headed, realistic man who does not believe in miracles, talismans or fate. But a chance encounter the next day in Paris airport got me rather excited, and left me with the feeling that this mission was starting with Fortune's blessings. While waiting for my flight to Zurich to be announced, I suddenly saw Danny Kaye. Danny Kaye, one of my favourite actors and performers, was standing not a metre away from me, waiting impatiently for his flight. I remember even today the casual clothes he wore, particularly the white socks that peeked out from between shoes and trousers, an American fashion which in those days was unknown and definitely unacceptable in Europe.

'I admire your great talent. Would you please sign your autograph for me?' I addressed him as I handed him a pen and an old flight ticket. Danny Kaye was evidently surprised by my request, but seemed pleased by the fact that he was a recognized celebrity even in Paris. He gladly granted my request.

A few hours later, with Danny Kaye's signature tucked deep in my pocket, next to US$6,000 in cash, I entered the cool, discreet and dimly lit chambers of the Credit Suisse Bank in the Paradeplatz in the centre of Zurich.

Money has no smell, definitely not in a bank in Switzerland, a country that has amassed its fortune through the discreet handling of finances that no one volunteers information about. I could not help wondering how many millions of Swiss francs or American dollars belonging to Nazi-persecuted Jews murdered in the concentration camps lay in the sparkling vaults of this bank, as well as in other Swiss financial institutions.

In the mid-1960s, US$6,000 was a handsome sum for the average employee, but from the professional point of view of the bank clerks who attended to my needs, and who were accustomed to handling unconventional clients such as cash couriers of dictators and Mafia bosses, this sum was merely 'small change'.

'According to your request, Herr Kuenzle, we have issued

a letter of credit under your name for the sum of US$6,000,' said the clerk, and put the document on the desk. 'And here is a list of Credit Suisse Bank representatives in Brazil, Argentina and Uruguay.'

In order to establish my position in Brazil, I asked the clerk to inform the Credit Suisse Bank representatives in those countries of the imminent arrival of an Austrian businessman by the name of Kuenzle, and to ask them to extend their assistance to him.

'No problem, Herr Kuenzle. Please consider it done,' replied the clerk.

Unlike in Israel, I knew that when a Swiss bank clerk told me to consider a matter done, it was indeed done. I had no doubt that the South American representatives of this bank would be notified of my arrival.

Since I had no further business in Zurich, I returned to Paris the same evening, and the following day went to have my passport photographs taken for my visa forms.

My moustache had not yet reached full maturity, and as time was of the essence, I employed a professional make-up artist to beef it up. I donned the heavy-rimmed glasses I had purchased in Rotterdam, and with a rather sombre expression, looked straight into the camera lens, and let the photographer immortalize Anton Kuenzle on celluloid. Had I known then, in September 1964, that half a year later this photo would feature prominently on Interpol posters below the headline, 'Wanted for Murder', I might have allowed a friendlier, even a smiling expression.

At the next coordinating meeting with Yoav and Michael, I demanded that another channel of communications be opened. I requested an additional channel to the PO box I had in Rotterdam, to which I could send my messages, a request which Yoav granted instantly. It was his policy to give his operational staff a free hand to act according to their understanding and experience, especially in such a case as mine, where I would have to be thousands of kilometres away from any other friendly agent, working on my own. I was given another post office box in Paris, which suited me just fine. All that was left now was to conclude my business in Holland.

Most of the passengers on the Trans-Europe Express from Paris to Rotterdam on Wednesday, 9 September were businessmen, and Anton Kuenzle fitted in perfectly among them. Immediately on arrival to Rotterdam, I went to the Brazilian Consulate, and handed in my visa request forms in triplicate along with my photographs. I also enclosed, of course, the medical certificate I had received the previous week, and presented the clerk with my Paris–Rio de Janeiro–Paris flight ticket, testifying to the fact that I had no intentions of settling in Brazil. In a few minutes the pages of my passport were adorned with the official stamp of the Brazilian Consulate in Rotterdam, authorizing a certain Anton Kuenzle to visit Brazil for the duration of three months.

I spent the rest of the day making rounds between those whose services I had employed the previous week.

At the tailor I tried on my suit, and was glad to see that it fitted me well, despite the roundness of my figure that set so many unexpected traps for the inexperienced tailor. I added a few elegant shirts to my pile, and left the store well-equipped for the Brazilian summer.

My personalized stationery, envelopes and business cards were ready at the printer's. All I needed now were travellers' cheques. I purchased those to the sum of US$1,000 at a nearby American Express office. I went over the list once more. The preparation stage was done. I packed all of my Rotterdam belongings, and returned to Paris.

I said goodbye to my wife, promising her that I would take care of myself, and would not endanger myself unnecessarily. The next day, in the evening hours of Friday, 11 September 1964, I boarded an Air France Boeing jet that took off with roaring engines into the night sky.

At the approximately same time, in far-away São Paulo, Herbert Cukurs was busy preparing his equipment, which included a seaplane and rental row and pedal boats, in anticipation of the weekend vacationers. He had no way of knowing that only a week ago some Israelis, 'those who shall never forget', had given him the title 'The Deceased'. Nor could he have known that with each kilometre this French plane full of passengers, among them the Austrian businessman Anton Kuenzle, flew toward its destination, the closer the moment approached in which this title, 'The Deceased', would be realized, and that his execution would become a sensation and make the headlines of newspapers around the world.

4
WHO WAS CUKURS?

'YOU ARE in great health and excellent condition. I wish you a pleasant flight, and a safe return home,' said Dr Weinreich to the air force captain who reported for a thorough physical at his clinic in Riga, the capital of Latvia.

The year was 1934. The medical was conducted as part of pilot Herbert Cukurs' preparations for his adventurous flight to Africa in a small fragile plane, the flight that was to turn him into a national hero in this small Baltic state.

When the respectable doctor, a member of the thriving Jewish community of Riga, and the brave pilot met again seven years later, there was no trace of the friendliness that had characterized their earlier encounter. The acclaimed doctor had become a persecuted Jew whose life was worth less than that of a dog or a roach. The pilot, Herbert Cukurs, on the other hand, had become the Angel of Death of Riga's Jews, and was about to annihilate the community that had been an inseparable part of the history of the city and of Latvia for hundreds of years.

A special ordinance dated 1645 earmarking a special inn for the Jewish merchants who frequented Riga is the first testimony to the presence of Jews in this Baltic town that in time would become the capital of Latvia. Jews were forbidden then to reside within the municipal boundaries of Riga, and it was only in the eighteenth century that a few merchant families were able to make their home in the town despite that ban.

From the beginning of the nineteenth century there was a steady growth in the number of Jews residing in Riga, and a community life started to form. In 1839, the Jews were given permission to establish a Jewish elementary school, one of the first in Russia. Two years later, in response to their mass migration there, the town again closed its gates to the Jews. In 1913, the Jewish community numbered 33,000, 6.5 per cent of the entire population. According to official data, one out of every five physicians in Riga was a Jew.

The history of Latvia's Jews in the twentieth century is a tale of sharp turns, painful changes and shifting circumstances, the result of an existence between the Russian hammer and the German anvil. German nationalists considered Latvia as an outpost of Germanic culture stranded deep inside the Slavic east. The landowners of most of Latvia were German noblemen, who controlled vast estates. The social elite was German. The language of Goethe and Schiller was the language of high culture, while the Russian language reached a similar status only after the repeated and relentless efforts of Czars Alexander the First and the Second to Russify Latvia.

Latvia was not only a swinging cultural pendulum, but also a disputed territory between Germany and Russia. During the First World War, the Germans occupied large parts of the Baltic lands, and in 1917, the year of the revolution, the German army took advantage of the breakdown in discipline in the Russian army, and took over Latvia completely.

In the 1918 Treaty of Brest-Litovsk Russia ceded Latvia to Germany. The imperial German flag flew over the government building of Latvia, but not for long. A few months later, one week after the fighting of the First World War came to an end, the Provisional National Council, headed by the Latvian nationalist Karlis Ulmanis, declared an independent Latvia. In response, the Red Army invaded Latvia. Ulmanis and his government fled to the port town of Libau, where they took refuge in the British Royal Navy warships anchored in the harbour. German combat troops led by General von der Goltz joined the turmoil, and chased the communists out of Riga. Independent Latvia was practically wiped off the map, then resurrected with the political and military help of Great Britain, France and Poland. The British and the French supported Ulmanis, and helped him drive out the Germans. The Polish army repelled the Red Army from the remaining parts of Latvia, and in 1920 this tumultuous chapter in the annals of the young state came to an end with the peace treaties Latvia signed with Germany and the Soviet Union.

The Jewish community thrived between the years 1920 and 1934, the democratic era of independent Latvia. The Jews took part in all facets of life, including politics. The politician Siegfried Meierowitz, who had never turned his back to his Jewish roots, served as the young state's foreign minister for quite a while. There were Jewish schools at all levels throughout Latvia, particularly in Riga, enjoying state and local municipal support. The official languages at these school were Yiddish, Hebrew and German.

Riga also hosted a Yiddish theatre of great acclaim. Three Jewish daily newspapers held bitter distribution battles, vying for readers, who, as is common in the Jewish world, were divided into many different camps: religious, secular, socialist, communist, conservative, Zionist, Bundist and others. The town hosted two prominent Jews during those years: the historian Simon Dubnov, and Rabbi Yitzhak Yosef Schneerson, who made Riga a temporary centre of the Chabad movement.

The global economic crisis of the 1930s hit not only Latvia's economy, but also the fabric of its democratic life. The citizens of Latvia, a motley crew of Latvians, Russians, Poles, Germans and Jews, were able to agree on almost nothing. For example, the 100 elected Parliament members, representing 24 different factions, blocked every possibility of governing the state.

Ulmanis, Latvia's War of Independence hero, took advantage of this fragile situation. He seized power in 1934 and, following Benito Mussolini's example, dissolved Parliament, forbade all party politics, and declared a cooperative government. The new regime imposed heavy restrictions on the cultural and religious autonomy of Latvia's Jews, half of which, approximately 30,000, resided in Riga.

Ulmanis' nationalist government immediately launched a Latvian heritage campaign. The term was in fact meaningless, but this did not deter the regime's followers from their frenzied activities. School curricula were adjusted to suit the party line, and history books were rewritten to reflect the new reality. They included, for instance, detailed descriptions – bereft of any historical basis – of the feats of the ancient tribes of Lettgals and Semgals, as well as of the heroic struggle of the different Latvian tribes against the German attempts to expand eastward. The idea behind it all was to emphasize the contribution of the ancient Latvians to the formation of modern Latvia.

Amidst all this excitement, Captain Herbert Cukurs had an amazing idea that actually embodied the absurdity and ridiculousness of the rewriting of history Ulmanis and his followers had undertaken – a daredevil flight from Latvia on the shores of the Baltic Sea to distant Gambia, in western Africa, on the shores of the Atlantic Ocean. Now, what on earth could be the connection between Latvia and Gambia?

It all began in the sixteenth century with a commercial enterprise initiated by a nobleman from a well-known family who owned vast lands in what had later become Latvia. Hearing of the phenomenal gains that awaited anyone who set foot on the newly discovered distant continents, he decided to join the fray. He purchased a large expanse of land in western Africa, in today's Gambia, and established a trading post there. The business adventure of the aristocrat from the far north collapsed after a short while. It failed to compete against the business acumen of the Dutch, English and Portuguese tradesmen, who were more adaptable to the harsh reality of equatorial Africa.

This brief episode of Latvian commercial involvement in the era of exploration vanished in the dustbin of history without a trace, until the time when a few historians, staunch supporters of Latvia's new regime, discovered this long-forgotten affair while digging through old archives. Nothing stood in the way of the Latvian nationalists to slightly rewrite history and recruit this event to serve the glory of the tiny state, not even the fact that the failed businessman in question was none other than the German Duke Jakob of the renowned Kettler family.

Cukurs, a pilot in the country's small air force, an aeronautic engineer by training, and an avowed nationalist, heard of this discovery, and decided that a flight from Latvia to Gambia in the small biplane he had designed would abridge hundreds of years of Latvian history and glorify the name of the small country. His suggestion received the enthusiastic support of the regime, and the generous financial backing of Latvia's most popular newspaper, the *Jaunakas-Zinas*. It is worth mentioning here that the 1920s and 1930s were the golden era of civil aviation, when flight pioneers became folk heroes, such as Charles Lindbergh who was the first pilot to fly across the Atlantic without stopping. Cukurs' idea matched the spirit of the time, not to mention the regime's aspirations. Thus, in 1934, Cukurs set out on his pioneering flight along the somewhat odd route, Latvia to Gambia.

Every mile logged by Cukurs' little plane received enthusiastic coverage by the Latvian press, as if it were an event of historical proportions, as well as a turning point in the history of aviation. No wonder, therefore, that when he returned from his long flight, Cukurs became overnight a national hero and an acclaimed personality. The 'Baltic Lindbergh' was but one of the names given to this adventurer. The Latvian government's highest honour, and the highly respected international aviation decoration, the Order of Santos Dumont, named after the Brazilian aviation pioneer, were pinned to his chest. Cukurs' light plane was placed in the war museum, and every self-respecting Latvian citizen joined the long queue at the museum's entrance. A poster on the wall reminded the visitors of the long flight and provided them with biographical details of its pilot.

Herbert Cukurs was born on 17 May 1900, in the small town of Libau. His family, who were farmers, moved into town, where his father Janis opened a machine shop. As a youth and later as a young soldier, Cukurs witnessed the failed battles Ulmanis launched against the Red Army, and his hasty flight to Libau, where he found shelter behind the 16-inch-calibre guns of the British navy. Cukurs took part in Latvia's struggle for independence, serving in the young state's meagre air force. During his military service, Cukurs befriended other officers who held nationalist ideas similar to his own. However, Cukurs' military career did not soar, and he was discharged as a captain. The former officer did not hide his nationalistic views and, as was the custom among military circles, he also made the occasional anti-Semitic remark. But this was nothing extraordinary, and he was not really considered a Jew-hater. The opposite was true, since he was often seen in Riga's cafés in the company of Jewish intellectuals.

Following his flight to Gambia, the daring pilot became a household name in Latvia, a true celebrity. The country's most popular newspaper, which had sponsored his flight, offered him a position, and once more Cukurs set out on long flights. He flew to Japan, over Turkey, and to British Mandate Palestine, sending lengthy and detailed feature articles from wherever he happened to land.

'I remember well Cukurs' lecture at the Jewish club in Riga,' says Professor Yoel Weinberg, a Riga-born Biblical historian who immigrated to Israel in 1993, still speaking the fluent Hebrew he had learned at high school in the years that preceded the war. 'Cukurs' lecture took place in 1937,' he recalls. 'The entire Jewish elite of Riga gathered in the elegant club in Skolas Street, in order to listen to the journalist-cum-pilot's impressions of his visit to the Land of Israel. The lecture hall was packed with hundreds of people. I remember Cukurs speaking with wonderment, amazement, even with enthusiasm, of the Zionist enterprise in Israel. He accompanied the lecture with photographs he himself had taken, which were projected onto a large screen. There were pictures of Tel-Aviv and of the then settlements of Petah Tikvah and Rishon Letzion. I had been studying at a Hebrew school at the time, and Cukurs' tales fired my imagination. We spent the following day in class discussing the things Cukurs had said.'

Jews from Libau who knew the Cukurs family say that Herbert's hatred for the Jews did not come from his parents' home. 'Janis Cukurs and his wife were decent, honest folks,' says Meir Deutsch who, as a young man in the 1930s, worked with three other young Jews as apprentices in Herbert's father's machine shop. 'Janis Cukurs had four sons. I knew three of them quite well, Theodore, Edgar and Orward. They were decent people, they even had a warm attitude toward the Jews. But about Herbert I have nothing good to say.'

In the late 1930s Herbert Cukurs excelled in his activities in 'Perkonkrust' (Thunder Cross), a fascist organization led by Major Victor Arajas. This, however, did not stop him from maintaining ties with his Jewish acquaintances, and even lecturing to the Jewish community about the wonders of the new Jewish community in the Land of Israel, then Palestine.

Following 20 years of sovereignty, Latvia lost its independence in the summer of 1940. As part of the Molotov-Ribbentrop non-aggression pact that had been signed the previous year, which divided the spheres of influence in eastern Europe between Nazi Germany and Stalinist Soviet Union, the Red Army took over the Baltic states of Lithuania, Estonia and Latvia. Within hours of the takeover, a communist government was established, resting on Red Army bayonets. This government arrested Ulmanis, and declared new elections with the participation of one single party – the Communist Party.

Following these elections, on 5 August 1940 the new Parliament declared, the annexation of Latvia to the Soviet Union. The small Baltic country had once more been wiped off the political map, to which it returned only 50 years later, following the collapse of the Soviet Union. For Latvia's Jews, this brief communist period was characterized by an inconsistent mixture of persecution and privileges.

The commissars who came from Moscow ordered the closure of all the political organizations of Latvia's Jews, except for the communists of course. At the same time, though, they supported Jewish cultural life. The communists established a state Jewish education system that included ten elementary and three high schools in which studies were conducted in Yiddish. They also abolished the quota system for Jews in higher education, and their numbers doubled in comparison to previous years. The number of Jews in law school soared from 3 per cent to more than 20.

On the other hand, where the economy was concerned, the communist regime brought about a deterioration in the circumstances of Jewish life. The new government took over and nationalized industrial plants, commercial enterprises and banks which were under Jewish ownership. Yet many of those owners remained in the boardrooms as professional managers and advisors to the state-appointed commissars.

The annexation of Latvia to the socialist paradise also forced observant Jews to work on the Sabbath and Jewish holidays, which contravenes the religion's dictates and tradition. In at least one case, observant Jews came up with an original solution to this problem – a group of them established a cooperative of mattress manufacturing, which was always closed one day each week for taking inventory; somehow this day always fell on the Sabbath.

The Molotov-Ribbentrop non-aggression pact concerned not only politics, but also regulated the commercial trade between the two dictatorships. It may well have happened that as part of trade agreements with Germany, the products of Jewish textile workers working in plants that were under Jewish management were sent to the Wehrmacht, the German army, and to the evil SS units that were already busy persecuting the Jews of Poland and other countries that were under Nazi occupation. Rumours of the Nazi atrocities against the Jews of Poland reached the Baltic states. But most of Latvia's Jews were convinced that the German–Russian non-aggression pact guaranteed their safety, and that they would never witness Nazi army columns goose-stepping through the streets of Riga. Joseph Stalin was also convinced that he was in control of the situation, and that he understood his ally Adolf Hitler's ways of thinking and operating. But all of this blew up in the early morning hours of 22 June 1941. On Stalin's desk in the Kremlin lay many intelligence reports on the German army's intensified preparations for a full frontal attack. In at least two cases Soviet agents – Richard Sorge in Tokyo, and members of the Red Orchestra, a Jewish communist underground operating mainly in Belgium – passed on the exact date of the attack. But Stalin discarded all these reports, although his suspicion grew when the British passed on a similar warning. At this point he became convinced that this was nothing but an imperialist

British provocation, aimed at sabotaging the close relations with Nazi Germany.

While these reports amassed in Moscow, Riga's Jewish community was in uproar. On 14 June 1941, the internal security organ, the NKVD, deported more than 35,000 Latvians to distant Siberia. Among the deportees were approximately 5,000 Jews, most of them members of the various Zionist organizations, but also members of the orthodox organization Agudat Israel, Bundists of the non-Zionist Jewish socialist organization, and a group of Jewish businessmen and bankers. It is ironic that this inhumane deportation actually saved their lives.

One week later, and precisely as stated in the intelligence reports Stalin had discarded, the Nazi army launched a surprise attack along the entire front that stretched for thousands of kilometres. Columns of German tanks and armoured vehicles forged eastward at a rate of dozens of kilometres per day. Luftwaffe dive-bombers wrought havoc behind the lines. The Red Army retreated in disarray, leaving behind millions of prisoners of war.

On Tuesday, 1 July 1941, at midday, only a few hours after the Soviet army units who were bringing up the rear had left town, the Germans marched into Riga.

The Latvians welcomed the columns of soldiers goose-stepping through the picturesque streets of the Old City with flowers and cheers. They saw the Nazi soldiers as liberators from the hated communists, hoping that they would help them regain Latvia's independence. Latvian nationalists emerged from the underground, and openly joined units of the German army that was occupying their land. Some of the Latvian volunteers, members of the nationalist organization Aizsargi, had assisted the Germans in driving the Soviet troops out of Riga, and in seizing control of the radio stations, power plants, post offices and banks. But the German Nazis received the greatest help from the Latvian volunteers who belonged to the 'Perkonkrust', led by Victor Arajas and Herbert Cukurs. And while the German army was still busy clearing the last pockets of Soviet resistance, Arajas and Cukurs began to organize pogroms against the Jews of Riga.

SURVIVORS' EYEWITNESS TESTIMONIES

Testimony of Raphael Schub, 392 Clinton Street, Toronto, Canada. Appearing before the commission investigating Nazi crimes in the Baltic states. Testimony was given in Yiddish, in December 1949.

> Only three days after Riga's occupation by the German army on 1 July 1941, Cukurs started the annihilation of the Jews of Riga. On 2 July, Cukurs had already burned to death eight Jews in the new cemetery; the synagogue's officer Feldheim, his wife and four children, as well as the cantor Minz and his wife.
>
> In the early hours of 4 July, Cukurs started preparations for burning down the Great Synagogue on Gogol Street. On the first floor, in the vestibule of the synagogue, 300 Latvian Jews were gathered, having fled from nearby Liyk to Riga to seek asylum in the synagogue. Hauptmann [Captain] Cukurs and his men entered the synagogue and ordered the Jews to open the holy ark and spread the Torah scrolls on the synagogue's floor. The Jews refused to do as ordered, and Cukurs beat many of them savagely. He then ordered his men to unload a gasoline barrel from one of their trucks and roll it into the synagogue. They poured it all over the floor. Cukurs posted armed guards at all the synagogue doors and windows, and threw a hand grenade into the gasoline-soaked place. A huge fire broke out, and Cukurs' guards shot at the petrified Jews who scrambled to the doors and windows trying to escape the burning building. All 300 Jews inside the building, among them many children, burned to death.
>
> *Signature of Raphael Schub*

Testimony of Abraham Shapiro, 23 Waechter Street, Munich. Given before the legal department of the Organization of Liberated Jews in Germany, on 19 December 1949.

> The witness was 16 years old when the German army conquered Riga in the summer of 1941. On 2 July 1941,

accompanied by a few aides and soldiers, Cukurs forced his way into the apartment of the Shapiro family. He knew the head of the family, Pinkus Shapiro, from before the war. Cukurs told him that he was appropriating the apartment for his personal use, and instructed all the Shapiro family members to immediately evacuate the place. The head of the family pleaded with Cukurs personally, asking him for mercy. Cukurs remained impervious, and the father was taken to the central jail in Riga. When a few days later the mother of the witness tried to find out what had happened to her husband, Cukurs checked the lists in his hand, and indifferently informed her that her husband had been executed. The witness related that he was taken to the Latvian police headquarters at 19 Waldemar Street, and was employed doing menial jobs in the cellar of the building. In the cellar were approximately 100 tiny cells, filled with Jewish detainees.

'I witnessed Cukurs abuse the detainees. Many times I saw Cukurs and his men load hundreds of Jews on their trucks. We were instructed to bring shovels and spades to the trucks. The trucks returned empty four or five hours later. The shovels were dirty with dust and soil, and also with blood stains. One day, all the inmates in the cells were called to attend a roll-call. I worked with a Jew called Lutrin. All the Jews indeed attended the roll-call, except the two who hid with us: one was called Leitmann, but I no longer remember the name of the other. The one responsible for the detainees informed Cukurs that four Jews failed to report as instructed. Lutrin and I explained to Cukurs that we had been busy cleaning his car, but the two other Jews had no excuse or explanation. Cukurs instructed the guards to beat the two terribly, and then pulled out his gun and shot them dead. Cukurs knew that I played the piano well, and one day summoned me to the apartment he had appropriated from my parents. Cukurs ordered me to play for him and his guests, all of them high functionaries in the Latvian police. I saw how they brought a Jewish girl into the room, and how those present abused her. As I was playing, I saw how the Latvians forced the girl to undress and how they sexually abused her. I know that the girl was held prisoner in the apartment for many weeks.

Signature of Abraham Shapiro
Signature of Legal Department

Testimony of Max Tukacier, born in Riga on 1 August 1902, 22 Waechter Street, Munich. Given before the legal department of the Organization of Liberated Jews in Germany, on 23 September 1949.

I lived in Riga since the day I was born. I knew Herbert Cukurs personally since 1928. He too was a Latvian citizen. He is about my age, give or take. Cukurs was a sportsman, and became famous in Latvia because of the flights he made to Gambia, which is in Africa. On 1 July 1941 the Germans conquered Latvia. Cukurs immediately became one of the central and leading figures in the Nazi organization 'Thunder Cross', which immediately following the occupation established its headquarters at 19 Waldemar Street, in the home of the famous Jewish banker Schmulian. Jews were attacked in the streets, and driven out of their homes. Cukurs' people apprehended Jews in the streets, and brought them to their headquarters on Waldemar Street. I too was apprehended in the street, on 15 July, and thrown into a cellar where about 200 Jews were held, men and women. Cukurs and his men, 20 in all, were masters of our fate. On Cukurs' instructions, every few minutes a group of ten Jews was taken to the offices above. We heard how they were beaten, and we also heard shots.

Every 15 or 20 minutes another group of ten people was taken from the cellar. I belonged to the seventh group Cukurs and his men brought up. We were brought to a large room. Articles of clothing and shoes were scattered in the corners of the room. The Latvians led by Cukurs gave us a horrible beating. Cukurs commanded the scene, and with the butt of his weapon beat people on their heads and on other parts of their bodies. Cukurs hit me in the face and broke almost all of my front teeth.

Cukurs ordered us to take our clothes off and stand facing the wall, and then he noticed we were 11 and not 10, as he had ordered. He told his policemen to take down the superfluous one. Since I stood at the end of the line, and nearest to the stairs down to the cellar, I was sent back, accompanied by four Latvians, who beat me fiercely. At that moment I heard many shots.

About half an hour later Cukurs and his escorts appeared in the cellar. There were bloodstains on their clothes. 'Everybody upstairs!' Cukurs shouted, and the first group, 20 men and I among them, was shoved upstairs. We were brought to the same large hall where I had been earlier, and were ordered to arrange the clothes of those who had been shot. The Latvian SS men brought buckets full of water and ordered us to wash the bloodstains off the walls and floor of the hall.

We were then pushed into the yard. At that moment hundreds of Jews who were brought from town entered the yard. Cukurs instructed that we be taken far into the yard, in order to avoid any contact between us and them. Around the corner, beneath a large window, we noticed a pile of naked and almost naked bodies. At that moment we understood that these were the bodies of the Jews who had been brought up from the cellar.

Suddenly Cukurs came close. He saw that we had noticed the bodies, and ordered us to turn away. Following a brief consultation with his policemen, I heard one of them say to him: 'It's not so terrible, soon they'll also be part of this pile.' And so we stood there for about an hour with our backs turned to the bodies. Cukurs warned us not to turn our faces to the bodies. But since we had already seen death before our eyes, two of our group turned their heads around anyway, and the Latvian policemen killed them with shotguns. One of the murdered was Chaim Leibowitz, but I don't know the name of the other.

We were brought up to the hall, which was full of Jews. Then Cukurs appeared with his abettors, and they started beating people right and left, and abusing those in the hall... In this way Cukurs beat to death between 10 and 15 people, and I was an eyewitness to these deeds.

At Cukurs' orders, some of us were picked out, and we had to throw the dead bodies out through the window. At that stage Cukurs disappeared, and we were left with the Latvian SS people. We were chased into the yard, and there the beating and abuse resumed, and many more of us were beaten to death. A large group of people was separated from us, and later I found out that they were taken to the jailhouse. We had to stand on our feet all night long. On the following day, 16 July 1941, only about 40 people remained in the yard. The guards asked who wanted to volunteer for work, but since many did not believe that the talk was about real work, but rather about something else, only 30, and I among them, volunteered. We were taken to the building of the Ministry of the Interior, where we did the cleaning.

On 29 November the great *Aktion* took place in the ghetto. As we, about 30,000 Riga Jews, congregated in the central square of the ghetto, I saw Cukurs arrive in his car. He wore a long, beautiful leather coat. Cukurs was one of the commanders of the *Aktion*. Anyone who was declared fit for work or an expert was moved to another part of the ghetto, 'the little ghetto'. The rest, about 26,000 Jews, were returned to the ghetto. The next day, 30 November, at 6 o'clock in the morning, the Jews of the ghetto were gathered again in the square, and led in long columns to the Valley of the Dead in the Bikernieki Forest.

The columns passed in front of the 'little ghetto', and from my window I saw the Jews and their escort of Latvians and Germans, and Cukurs. Cukurs mercilessly beat and also shot many people who did not keep up with the pace of the march. There were men, women and children among his victims. This picture repeated itself when the rest of the Jews of the ghetto were brought to the Valley of the Dead on 7 and 8 December 1941.

Signature of Max Tukacier

Testimony of Michael Miron, previously Mironovitsch, 135 West 80 Street, New York.

I was born in Riga in 1908. I served in the air force of the Latvian navy in 1929 and 1930, or 1930 and 1931. Herbert Cukurs was an officer in the air force. This is how I know who he is.

I was living in Riga when the war broke out. The Germans occupied Riga at the beginning of July 1941. At the beginning of November the first *Aktion* took place, during which thousands of Jews were murdered, among them my wife and three children.

I myself was deemed fit for work. I lived in the ghetto but worked for the Germans, usually outside the ghetto. I heard from the Latvian policemen who guarded the exits of the ghetto that Cukurs was serving as an officer in the Latvian police, which collaborated with the Germans. From personal knowledge I know the following details about Cukurs: about a week after the first *Aktion*, another one took place. I returned from work to the ghetto. At the entrance to the ghetto I, together with the group I belonged to, received orders from a German policeman to clean the dead from the streets and take the bodies to the cemetery. The dead – these were the Jews who could not walk and were already shot to death inside the ghetto.

As I entered the ghetto with my group, Jews were still being driven out of their hiding places on Great Kalna Street. There I saw with my own eyes Cukurs riding on his horse. He was dressed in Latvian uniform, held a gun in his hand, and was shooting at the hunted Jews. He shot many. I saw the Jews falling dead.

I can testify as a witness that Cukurs rode a horse and shot Jews to death. I had heard no command ordering Cukurs or anybody else to shoot.

Signature of Michael Miron before notary Irving Friedman
New York, 1 August 1960

Testimony of Sonya Bider, born Kalmanovitsch in Riga, 23 May 1918

> One Sunday, soon after the first great *Aktion*, on 29 or 30 November, about 300 other women and I who were designated as seamstresses were brought to the jail. One of the friendlier local guards told me in Latvian: 'You are the lucky ones.'
>
> The next day the door opened with a lot of noise, and in the entrance stood Herbert Cukurs with a few more people. He held in his hand a large whip which had a piece of metal on the end. Without reason or warning, he started lashing the women who were close to the door until they bled. With the help of whip lashes, he divided us into two groups of about 150 women each. One group stayed in jail, and the other was taken back to the ghetto. The 150 women who were sent back to the ghetto were murdered. About two weeks later the group of 150 women who remained in jail was taken back to the ghetto, and I with them. The ghetto was now almost completely vacant, and under the direct control of the German police.
>
> I decided to give this testimony of my own free will and without any external pressure, after having read in the newspapers that Herbert Cukurs, who was mentioned above, presented himself to the Brazilian official authorities as a humane man, and as someone who had helped Latvian Jews during the Nazi occupation. As can be seen from the encounter I had with Cukurs, the very opposite is true.
>
> *Tel-Aviv, 10 October 1960*
>
> *Signature of Sonya Bider*

Testimony of Isaak Kram, 255 Washington Avenue, New York.

> I was born in Riga in 1921, and finished my studies at the Hebrew High School of Riga. I was a student of construction engineering at the university when the Germans occupied Riga at the beginning of July 1941.

Two Latvian policemen arrested my father at the end of July. He was taken to the jail, and we haven't seen him since. When the Jews were driven to the ghetto, we also moved there – my mother, my younger brother, my 9-year-old sister and me. My brother and I were often taken to do work outside the ghetto. At the end of November 1941 the first *Aktion* took place, that is, the women and children were taken elsewhere. At the end of work, my brother and I were not allowed to return to our apartment in the ghetto, and we were sent to another part of the ghetto. In the meantime, many women and children had been already deported from the ghetto, among them my mother and my younger sister. Later we found out that they had been murdered in the nearby forest.

About a week later, on 7 December, the second *Aktion* took place. My brother and I were not called up for work. I stood at the fence of Ludzas Street, in the 'little ghettos' quarter, and watched the Jews as they were being driven out through this street. Herbert Cukurs commanded the Latvian policemen and soldiers. They wore uniforms with green stripes on their arms. Cukurs was well known as a pilot. He wore a black military pilot's jacket, and over it a warm leather coat. I saw how he shot at Jews.

In the meantime I was recruited to clear away bodies from the road and bring them to the cemetery. This is how I got really close to Cukurs. An old Jewish woman screamed because her daughter was not allowed to climb with her onto the truck. Cukurs pulled out his gun and shot the old woman. I was an eyewitness to this shooting. I also saw with my own eyes how Cukurs aimed his gun at a baby who was crying because he could not find his mother. Cukurs killed that baby with a gunshot.

Signature of Isaak Kram

Testimony of David Fiszkin, born in Riga on 1 February 1921. Given before the legal department of the Organization of Liberated Jews in Germany.

> I know personally the war criminal Herbert Cukurs, because I was in Ghetto Riga, particularly on 30 November 1941, and I can say that we are dealing here with a great war criminal, a sadist, who is responsible for the death of hundreds of Jews.
>
> On 30 November, there was the great *Aktion* in the ghetto, and about 10,000 Jews were taken to the forest and killed there. The Germans were the ones who selected the Jews, and Cukurs accompanied them to the forest and took part in their murder. Many Jews could not keep up with the pace of the march, and Cukurs, who always brought up the rear, shot the stumblers without an explanation and for no reason. When a child was crying, Cukurs snatched him from his mother's arms and shot him to death. With my own eyes I saw how he shot and killed ten children and babies. I also saw eight cases in which he shot those who could not keep up the pace with the rest when they were still inside the ghetto. On that day, 30 November, Cukurs killed about 500 Jews who were on their way to the Valley of the Dead in the forest.
>
> I hereby confirm my oath and the truth of the details above, and am ready to appear as a witness before a court of law, and I am well aware of the consequences of perjury.
>
> *Signature of David Fiszkin*
> *10 October 1948*

Testimony of Otto Tuchel, an SS man who participated in the massacre of the Jews of Riga. Given at the City of Hamburg courthouse, where in December 1972, he, together with three other former SS men, stood trial.

> We marched the Jews to the forest. The victims, clad only in their underwear, were ordered to pass by the dead. The shots were not always deadly. The shooters sat on the edge of the mass grave and took turns shooting and drinking vodka from a bottle. Everything was over by lunch time. We returned to the guardroom in the ghetto – we only wanted to drink the brandy we

> deserved – and here came the commander and said that there were still 18 sick Jews who must be shot in front of the synagogue. Each of us would have to shoot one Jew. The calculation was spot on – we were 18 policemen.

* * *

The testimonies of the survivors of Herbert Cukurs' cruel atrocities – together with documents and newspaper cuttings – are kept in the Yad Vashem archives in Jerusalem, in four bulky cardboard files numbered 151 through 154. Many witnesses remember well the large Nagan handgun Cukurs used often, whether to beat to death his defenceless victims, or to murder women and children with shots at close range. The witness Dr Gerd Weinreich documented how Cukurs smashed the skulls of two babies he had snatched from their mothers' arms. Cukurs committed this atrocity at the Jewish Hospital of Riga, before the horrified eyes of Dr Weinreich, the very same doctor who seven years earlier had given him a thorough physical before his flight to Gambia.

At the same time as the Jews of Riga were being annihilated in the Rombula Forest, the Valley of the Dead, about eight kilometres away from the ghetto, the Germans brought into the ghetto thousands of 'German' Jews, Jews who had been driven out of the territories of the Third Reich. The German police assumed command of the ghetto, and restricted the authority of the Latvian volunteers lead by Arajas and Cukurs. Cukurs continued loyally to serve the Nazis in occupied Latvia not only during their victories, but even after the tide turned at the Battle of Stalingrad, and the Red Army opened a series of counterattacks that, in the spring of 1945, brought it to the centre of Berlin.

In October 1944, shortly before the Red Army liberated Riga, Cukurs and his family joined the retreating columns of the German army, together with approximately 70,000 other Latvians who feared acts of revenge by the advancing Russians. In addition to his possessions, he also took along with him an original 'life insurance policy' – a young Jewish woman whose life he had personally saved.

'I knew he had served in the SS, but I never heard that he was involved in the atrocities,' said the young woman,

Miriam Kaicner, in her testimony before the commission of inquiry of the Jewish organizations in Brazil, in 1950. 'Cukurs hid me for many weeks in Shapiro's apartment in Riga. Later, when we were brought to the ghetto, he saw to it that food would reach me. Later on he freed me from the ghetto, and brought me to his family's farm, where I stayed until the Russians came close to Latvia. He provided me with false documents, which helped me reach Berlin together with him. Cukurs fled Riga in a beautiful car, hauling a trailer full of expensive furniture and other property. He bartered small things from the trailer for fuel, and so we never had any problem moving on.

'In Berlin he got me a job at the airplane manufacturers, Brucker Flugzeugbau. He himself also worked in the factory as an engineer. Even before the Red Army took over Berlin, Cukurs succeeded in saving his family and me. We fled town in the car, with the trailer behind, and found refuge in a forest near the town of Kassel. We hid there for seven months, until we moved to France and settled temporarily in Marseilles. Cukurs started working in a small boat-rental business, yet continued to look for a safe place. With the help of Catholic organizations, we succeeded in obtaining entry visas to Brazil. Cukurs sold the car and the remaining possessions in the trailer, as well as his share in the boat-rental business. In the winter of 1946 we boarded the ship *Cape of Good Hope*, and on 4 March 1946 we reached Brazil.'

Herbert Cukurs presented himself in Brazil as a Latvian refugee, a farmer by profession, a victim of the communists, who had risked his own life in order to save a young Jewish woman.

The full circumstances of this inconceivable tie between the Hangman of Riga and one of his victims was never made clear. After having testified on behalf of Cukurs for three hours, Miriam Kaicner disappeared. According to rumours, she moved to Rio de Janeiro, and married a local Jew there. Since then she has disappeared without a trace.

Cukurs settled down in Rio de Janeiro, at 645A Barata-Ribeiro Street, and received Brazilian ID card number 217180. He believed he had reached safety, and perhaps also economic prosperity due to the small boat-rental business he established on one of the lakes near town – Lagoa Rodrigo de Freitas. These plans were ended abruptly when Holocaust survivors from Riga identified him. They raised an outcry, and with the assistance of Jewish organizations, tried to block Cukurs' appeal for Brazilian citizenship. The Brazilian Jews did not keep still, and one evening a couple of dozen young Jews stormed Cukurs' dock, wrought havoc, destroyed the equipment, and forced Cukurs and his family – his wife Milda, his sons Gunnar and Herbert, and his daughter Atinela – to leave Rio de Janeiro.

Cukurs moved to Niteroi, and tried to make a living from the nightclub he opened on a large boat. This business failed as well and Cukurs, who had already turned 50, sought the financial help of the banker Fredrico Mello, in order to establish a yacht club in the Bay of Jujuruba. But the series of business failures continued, and in 1957 Cukurs tried his luck in Santos, the port town of São Paulo. He opened an air-taxi company there, 'Herbert & Filhos', but this did not last long either. In the meantime, Brazilian Jews kept updating Cukurs' file and gathering details about his past.

'One day I was asked to obtain photographs and documents of the pilot Cukurs,' Riga-born Joseph Schneider related many years later. After the war he had stayed in Riga in order to help the remaining Jews immigrate to Israel. Using the papers of his brother, who had been a student of aeronautics, Schneider gained entry to Riga's central archives, ostensibly in search of aviation-related documents. He found many photographs from Cukurs' days of glory as a pilot in old newspapers and history books. 'I hid a tiny razor blade between my fingers, and very quickly cut out the photos from the history books and bound newspapers,' Schneider recalled. 'If there are today in Riga some damaged aviation books and volumes – it is because of me . . .'. Schneider sent the photographs to a Jew who lived in Rio de Janeiro with a brief letter that said 'Here are the photographs of your uncle.'

Three times Cukurs tried to become naturalized in Brazil. He even gave a sworn affidavit that he had had a son during his stay in Brazil, a fact that would have granted him the right to become a citizen. But the Jewish organizations thwarted all these attempts, claiming that the Brazilian-born child was most probably Cukurs' grandson. At the same time they kept urging the legal authorities to put Cukurs on trial for the atrocities he had committed during the war, or alternatively, to extradite him to Germany. To no avail, though.

'We are unable to extradite Cukurs to Germany since he was never a German citizen,' stated the official explanation. 'For the very same reason, the extradition request of the Soviet Union is also invalid. In addition, he cannot be extradited at all, since he is the father of a son who was born on Brazilian soil.'

The efforts to put Cukurs on trial peaked during the spring and summer of 1960, following the kidnapping of Adolf Eichmann in Argentina by Israeli Mossad agents.

'Latvia's Jews did everything in order to bring this murderer to trial,' reader Moshe Beilinson wrote in anger to the editor of the New York Yiddish newspaper *Der Tog Morgen*. In his letter, published on 27 July 1960, Beilinson emphasized the fact that he himself was a Holocaust survivor from Riga who had witnessed Cukurs' atrocities. 'The blood of the innocent Jews from Riga is screaming and demanding to put on trial the SS Hauptmann Herbert Cukurs, the Eichmann of Latvia,' Beilinson wrote. 'He must be apprehended before he vanishes, and it doesn't matter where it happens, in Brazil, Israel, or any other place.'

Cukurs felt threatened. The story of Eichmann's kidnapping scared him. He turned to the authorities and asked for their protection. The Brazilian secret service, the DOPS, guarded his home and gave him a license to carry a weapon for self-defence. The protection detail of Cukurs and his family was maintained even when, in 1961, they moved to São Paulo and settled down in the Interlagos area, on the shores of the artificial lake on the edge of town.

5
THE LIE OF THE LAND

'HOTEL CALIFORNIA, Avenida Atlantica 2616,' I told the taxi-driver at Rio's international airport, demonstrating a knowledge of the city in order to avoid a circuitous and expensive journey to my hotel.

Before climbing into the taxi I waved goodbye to my neighbour on the long flight from Paris, who had taught me a quick and vitally important lesson in Brazilian business practices. A few minutes before landing, as I looked on with amazement, he took a folded hundred-dollar bill and placed it inside his passport. 'If you run into problems with customs, come to me, I'll fix it,' he said.

I tried to follow the taxi's progress through the city and compare the sights I was seeing through the window with the ones I had seen from the plane just before landing. After all, Rio de Janeiro is considered one of the most beautiful cities in the world. But I was exhausted from the flight, and soon gave up my attempt, relying on the driver to bring me to my destination.

The view from the Hotel California's restaurant made me think of the more pleasant facets of my occupation, a partial compensation for the constant tension and danger. Copacabana Beach stretched outside in all its glory. It was a fairly wide strip of golden sand, bordering blue waters on one side, and strewn with myriad colourful dots that were in fact beautiful suntanned women clad in skimpy bathing suits that in some other countries in this period would have brought out the moral police in full force to raid the shore and drive away with wagonloads full of lovely detainees. The hundreds of kites in various colours and shapes, such as eagles, dragons and butterflies, that soared in the pleasant sea breeze, completed the picture of a free and easy life without a care in the world.

'Arrived safely. Love to everyone,' I reported to my friends in the two telegrams I sent to Rotterdam and Paris.

Over a plate of papaya – then a new and exotic fruit for me – pineapple and other juicy fruit, I planned my next moves. Since I had landed on the weekend, I decided to act like a common tourist and use the next couple of days to get acquainted with Rio and its surroundings. At the hotel reception desk, I booked a place on the 'Rio at Night' tour, and until the tour began, took a leisurely stroll through the city. In the evening, I joined a group of tourists led by an energetic tour guide, who introduced us to some of the sights, sounds and aromas of this beautiful town.

'Haste' is a dirty word in Brazil. There is plenty of time for everything, and it can be spent in one of the many little cafés, sipping piping hot and sweet *cafezinhos*, and holding endless discussions on any topic in the world provided it leads to politics or football.

I was also amazed at the great number of children's stores, be it clothing or toys. 'We Brazilians love children,' explained the guide as if on cue. 'Even the poorest families will insist on having a magnificent christening, even if they have to mortgage their future for it. They say that two kinds of businesses will never go under in Brazil – children's clothing stores and toy stores.'

The guide took us on the regular round along the beaches and through the centre of the city, and did not forget to point out the memorial monument to the 467 Brazilian soldiers who were killed in Italy during the Second World War. He also showed us the enormous Maracana Stadium, and Sugar Loaf Mountain. He organized a group photograph on top of Corcovado Mountain, the city's other famous mountain. As we stood atop the 700-metre-high peak beneath the outstretched arms of the statue of Jesus that is 1,400 tons of concrete and granite and 30 metres high, one of the most beautiful cities in the world spread before us.

In the early 1960s, before the era of mass tourism, a tour like ours also included a visit to the *favelas*, the terrible slums, where approximately a quarter of Rio de Janeiro's population lived. It was an unplanned mess of corrugated iron and wooden shacks, without electricity or running water. The fact that epidemics did not break out there every other day could not have been attributed to Rio's public health system, which had never excelled itself, but to the tens of thousands of Urubu vultures nesting in the neighbourhood. These birds ate almost everything, except for plastic and metal, and so prevented an outbreak of rodents, commonly responsible for spreading diseases and epidemics.

A few months before my arrival in Brazil, the army deposed the leftist President Jaoa Goulard, and replaced him with Marshal Umbertto Castelo Branco. Since then the police and army were omnipresent in Rio de Janeiro, and the streets, even of the *favelas*, were relatively safe.

Our guide took us to see a real *macumba* ceremony. We entered a large hut, lit only by candlelight. The ceremony, which dated back to the slavery period and whose origins were in Africa, was led by an elderly woman. Under her guidance, and to the ceaseless, rhythmic beating of the drums, the participants gradually went into a trance of wild dancing and bewitched movements. With their eyes closed, white froth coming out of their mouths, they turned round and round to the rhythm that grew faster and louder, until they collapsed on the ground, writhing in convulsions. This was a real Voodoo ceremony, not a show for tourists – a rare experience I could never forget.

The next day I joined a different group of tourists, going with them to Petropolis, a mountainous recreation area surrounded by forests, where Rio's rich took refuge on hot days. In the nineteenth century, when Emperor Dom Pedro the Second ruled Brazil, he built there a magnificent palace in the centre of the town. It had been turned into a museum, and its centrepiece was the crown studded with 600 diamonds and dozens of pearls that the emperor donned on official occasions.

We had lunch at a hotel restaurant in town, and as we tackled a *feijoada*, a typical Brazilian casserole made of black beans and pieces of meat, I suddenly discovered a sign saying that the place was run by the Santa-Paula-Melhoramentos Company. I was familiar with this name from the files I had studied before leaving for Brazil, which mentioned that not long ago this company had started to build a yacht club in Interlagos, near São Paulo, not far from Herbert Cukurs' boat-rental dock. This immediately triggered my operational instincts, even though I was on a tour that was ostensibly meant to foster my cover story as Anton Kuenzle.

What fortunate coincidence, I thought. One never knows what an innocent tour can turn up. Now I can get one step nearer to Cukurs, I thought, and without a second thought, knocked on the hotel manager's door.

The friendly manager was only too glad to talk about recreation and business with the visitor who had introduced himself as a colleague in the tourist industry. He provided me not only with brochures, but also with some details of his colleagues working in the company's headquarters in São Paulo.

'Go there. Tell them I sent you,' he urged.

I thanked him, and promised I would deliver his warmest regards to his friends if I ever went to São Paulo.

The following day, I sealed my stay in Rio by taking an important step to cement my cover story. I went to the tourist ministry of the local government – Brazil is a federal republic of 24 states – and introduced myself as a potential investor in the tourist trade. Not many minutes passed before I was deeply sunk in an elegant soft sofa in the local tourism minister's office. The honourable minister did everything he could to impress the entrepreneur from Europe, even bringing in the director general of his ministry for support. At the end of our meeting, the two furnished me with their business cards and a list of addresses that would be helpful in my future endeavours.

It's time to get closer to the target, I decided following this meeting. On to São Paulo! The flight to São Paulo left from the domestic flights airport, named after the flight pioneer Santos Dumont, who also gave his name to the respectable medal that in the 1930s had been pinned to Cukurs' chest in appreciation of his adventurous flight to Gambia and his achievements in developing Latvia's civil aviation.

I adapted myself quickly to the move from beautiful Rio de Janeiro to São Paulo, the business centre of Brazil. São Paulo already had a population of more than 5 million residents. The vast city spread over 650 square kilometres, a jungle of concrete, asphalt roads, skyscrapers and slums.

I checked into the Othon Palace, a comfortable and respectable hotel in the centre of town where most of the other guests were businessmen like myself, and then spent the next few days further establishing my cover story. To the outsider these activities may seem dull and unimportant, but my experience had taught me that it was precisely these activities that were vital for the successful completion of the mission I had undertaken, and for which I crossed the ocean and came to Brazil as Anton Kuenzle.

First I went to the local representative of my Swiss bank, Crédit Suisse, to find out whether my letters of introduction had arrived from Zurich. Then I went to the bank that represented Crédit Suisse in São Paulo, and inquired how I could withdraw money. At all of these places I left my business card, of course, and made sure that whoever I spoke with would remember my face. One day, if Cukurs, or anybody else for that matter, were to inquire whether a businessman by the name of Anton Kuenzle existed, had capital to invest, withdrew and deposited money, they would find plenty of evidence.

I ran all my errands in a rented orange VW Beetle, which came with a special Brazilian twist – a driver! It was rather odd to be chauffeur-driven in this tiny car, but Brazilian law required it. At that time, foreigners holding a driving license from another country or even an international driving license were not allowed to drive in Brazil without a special permit. So I went to the local motor vehicle office, and exchanged my driving license for a Brazilian document full of stamps and signatures, declaring me fit to manoeuvre a steering wheel on the roads of Brazil without the assistance of a local driver. I took leave of my driver, and thanked him for the lessons he had given me in 'surviving the roads of Brazil', which included a lesson on how to deal with the traffic police. When we were once stopped by such a traffic policeman, my driver just handed him 50 cruzeiros.

'It's not as if I've done anything wrong,' the driver had explained, 'but this is how it is here. Policemen must also make a living. You had better know, though, that from you, a foreign tourist, they would expect at least 500 cruzeiros, or else they'll give you trouble.'

Later that day I paid a visit to the offices of the Santa-Paula-Melhoramentos construction company, where I presented the business card of the hotel manager in Petropolis. It paved the way to an immediate meeting with the company's director and publicity and public relations manager. They responded to all my questions with courtesy and interest, and even provided me with a reference letter to the engineer in charge of the yacht club project in Interlagos, whose harbour, as it happened, bordered on Cukurs' dock.

I was pleased with my achievements. Thanks to the combination of plenty of professional experience and a little luck, I had managed in just four days to not only further establish my cover story and add concrete details to the character Anton Kuenzle, but also to get elegantly closer to the target without leaving any incriminating traces behind. Each step that brought me closer to Cukurs' dock, and to the inevitable face-to-face encounter with him, was the result of retraceable, logical and gradual acts that would appear natural and innocent even to the most suspicious person. If Cukurs did indeed decide to follow closely every step of mine, he would have to reach the conclusion that our meeting was a matter of pure coincidence. He would have to rule out the possibility that this was some well-planned operation aimed solely at trapping him. Feeling good, I sent my report to Rotterdam and Paris.

The following day, Thursday, 17 September, I drove my orange VW Beetle to the yacht harbour, to meet the engineer responsible for the project. I was a real pest and bombarded him with endless questions, but he was very patient, and I achieved my goal – he would remember me very well.

From the yacht harbour, which was under advanced construction, I let my eyes wander to Cukurs' dock and the surroundings. I noticed a thatched-roof restaurant with large windows facing Cukurs' dock. I said a warm goodbye to the engineer, who undoubtedly was happy to be rid of the curious and bothersome visitor, and casually wandered into the restaurant. I chose a table overlooking the lake, sat down and ordered a cold drink. Cukurs' dock was right before my eyes. There was a small quay, with row and paddle boats tied to it. A single-engine seaplane gently rocking in the water was also tied to the quay. Closer to the waterline stood a small hut that served as a makeshift ticket office. A young man, presumably one of Cukurs' sons, was busy doing maintenance work on the boats. I committed all these details to memory, and thought of how to proceed. 'Haste is from the devil', says a wise Arab proverb – and it suited my situation well. I must be careful not be too noticeable, I thought. Cukurs has been on the run for many years now, and there was no reason to jeopardize the operation only because of undue haste. One day more or less made no difference at the moment. According to the engineer I had just left, the entire Interlagos shore was teeming with life on the weekends. I could come back on Saturday and, blending into the general lively activity, get even closer to the target. But for now, this was enough.

I paid for the cold drink, climbed into the VW, and drove back to my hotel. On Friday I took a pleasant trip to Santos, São Paulo's harbour town. I toured the San Vicente quarter, where the Portuguese had established the first town in the new country, which they called Brazil, after the rosewood that was then used to produce a red dye for clothes. I enjoyed wandering into small restaurants, where I would sample the delicious local dishes. I quenched my thirst with endless and unusual juices. The Brazilians squeeze juice out of any fruit, even avocado, with very tasty results. I even learned to distinguish between the water-based *succo* juices, and the milk-based *vitaminas* juices. In the evening I returned to São Paulo, and spent the night writing a detailed letter in invisible ink, summing up all the information I had gathered so far. I also mentioned my future plans and signed with the usual request, to send my love to my family.

6
FIRST CONTACT

A PLATEFUL OF steaming fresh oysters in marinade landed on my table. I had ordered them following the waiter's recommendation as the 'spécialité de la maison'. They were delicious, and I enjoyed them thoroughly as I looked out of the restaurant window at the grass lawn that rolled gently to the shores of the artificial lake and to Cukurs' dock.

The place swarmed with weekend vacationers. The weather was fine, not too hot, with clear skies and a light breeze. Thousands of São Paulo's residents were taking advantage of the weekend to escape to the shores of this vast water reservoir, a popular recreation site.

The screams of joy of the people boating and swimming in the lake penetrated the restaurant. After half an hour of observation I concluded that at least during the weekend the Cukurs' family cash register did not stop ringing, and that the family members had very little spare time between Fridays and Mondays.

Following my meal, I strolled down the path that led to the lake, befittingly for a middle-aged man with a pot belly who had just consumed a dozen juicy oysters and was taking a slow stroll to aid the digestion.

'Hello ma'am,' I said in English to the young woman who sat behind the till in the small hut that served as the ticket booth. 'Do you speak English or French by any chance?'

The young woman, in her twenties, pretty, slender, with auburn hair and clear eyes, inspected me closely.

'You can speak German to me,' she replied in German, and smiled haltingly, glad to have recognized my Teutonic accent.

I introduced myself as a businessman checking out investment opportunities in the tourist trade in the region, and proceeded to pose a series of questions: How come she speaks German? How many customers do they have per day? How many boats do they operate? When is their peak season? Is there a peak season, or do vacationers come all year round? And so forth.

The young woman, who was, I found out later, married to one of Cukurs' sons, was not overwhelmed by my barrage of questions. She told me that she was originally from Dresden, the pretty German town that had been almost razed to the ground by the allied forces in February 1945, and that was in 1964 part of communist East Germany. Despite her best intentions, though, the young woman was unable to answer my specific professional questions.

'Do you see that tall man, with the white hair?' she asked, and pointed to the dock, where a man was busy tying up a seaplane to a pole. 'He's much more knowledgeable about such things than I. Talk to him. I'm sure he'll be helpful.'

I noticed during our conversation that she was looking with great interest at the ballpoint pen that stuck out of my shirt pocket. In the mid-1960s ballpoint pens were quite a novelty, having just been invented in the United States, and still on their voyage of global conquest.

'I see you like my pen. It is a Pelikan, made in Germany. Allow me to give it to you, as a memento from our homeland.'

The young woman did not know how to thank me. I, however, won myself an ally in the Cukurs' family, someone who would tell over dinner of my courtesy and generosity.

As I turned and walked away, she called after me, 'By the way, he speaks German, too.' I strolled toward the older man. From afar I could already recognize him. He was Herbert Cukurs, the Hangman of Riga. He was clad in a pilot's overalls, wore heavy-rimmed glasses and, despite his advanced age of 64, stood upright, accentuating his athletic figure.

'Good day,' I addressed him in German.

'A good day to you, too,' he responded calmly in German with a slight unidentifiable accent. Through his thick glasses he inspected me from head to toe.

'My name is Anton Kuenzle, and I'm a businessman. The friendly young lady at the ticket booth referred me to you.

I'm interested in the tourist trade here, and she told me you're an expert on this subject.'

Cukurs' response was curt, as if to say, look here, I'm busy at the moment, and have no time for silly chitchat.

I changed my approach, hoping that the opportunity to make a few cruzeiros would make him a little friendlier. 'I hear you fly tourists over the city. Perhaps you could take me for a flight over São Paulo?'

'With pleasure,' said Cukurs, who suddenly became friendly, especially once we agreed on the price, which, incidentally, was not exorbitant.

'My name is Cukurs, please board the plane.'

I am no expert on planes, but with hindsight, my hasty decision to get into this airplane bordered on complacent negligence and total disregard of any security measures. Cukurs' plane looked more like a metal tub with wings, engine and propeller. The cockpit was tiny, and the plane could carry only two passengers.

I took one of the two empty seats, and Cukurs started the engine. The plane emitted a cloud of acrid, blue smoke. The propeller turned slowly at first, haltingly, until it rotated at a steady speed. The noise was deafening, but at least it held an even pitch, indicating regular, good maintenance. Cukurs sailed slowly to the centre of the lake and, having ascertained that the water strip ahead was free of boats and swimmers, throttled the engine. After a few hundred metres of acceleration, accompanied by water splashing everywhere and the loud sound of the roaring engine and waves crashing against the hollow metal body, the plane lifted off from the water, and we were in the air.

No, I was not afraid to fly with the Hangman of Riga. Cukurs was an excellent pilot. He moved with great dexterity, and one did not have to be an aviation expert to recognize that the man had great technical skills and lived, loved and breathed airplanes. He clearly had vast experience in flying all sorts of airplanes, including this seaplane that had undoubtedly seen better days.

For approximately 20 minutes we flew over São Paulo and its surroundings. There was a light haze over the industrial areas. A thin layer of smog hovered over the centre of this city that stretched almost all the way to the horizon. Cukurs attempted to describe the sights below, but the noisy engine blocked any possibility of dialogue. And so, the first minutes of my acquaintance with Cukurs were characterized by heads nodding and were restricted to the occasional brief remark. The flight passed quickly. Cukurs circled over the city one more time, and turned the plane's nose back to the lake. The descent seemed a bit steep to me, but once we reached a low altitude over the water, Cukurs straightened the plane and landed smoothly on the lake, leaving behind a white wake like a speedboat. He navigated the plane expertly back to the dock, where one of his sons waited for us. Cukurs slid open a side window and threw out a rope which the young man tied to a pole.

'That was an extraordinary experience. I thoroughly enjoyed myself,' I thanked him, and once more posed a series of questions regarding tourism and investment opportunities in the Interlagos area.

'Could I invite you to my boat?' Cukurs asked, not concealing his pleasure over my compliments. 'I shall be only too glad to answer all of your questions in details over a glass of fine brandy.'

We entered the cabin of one of the larger boats that ferried tour groups. Cukurs produced a bottle of local brandy and two glasses, and generously poured the ochre liquid into them.

'*Prost*,' he toasted.

'*Prost*,' I responded.

'So what is it you want to know about tourism in Interlagos?' asked my host.

Once again I started with my litany of questions.

He said a couple of sentences, then gave me a piercing look. 'I'm accused of being a war criminal,' he said suddenly, and stopped, waiting for my reaction.

I remained impassive.

'Me, a war criminal?' he broke the silence after a few seconds. 'I? After I saved the life of a Jewish girl and protected her during the whole war?'

I still did not react. It made Cukurs uneasy. Undoubtedly he had planned these two last sentences well, in an attempt to place me on the political map, right or left. To this day I cannot comprehend what made him think this was a good tactic. Perhaps he thought I was a former Nazi looking for a safe haven. During that period the press was full of reports on the public debate surrounding the issue of the Statute of Limitations on Nazi war crimes. Many of these reports told of former Nazis who were deserting Europe in droves and moving to the safety of South America, fearful of having to stand trial in their home country.

I remained impassive, and Cukurs adopted a new tactic.

'Did you serve in the war? I'm sure you did,' he stated. He saw no need to specify which side he thought I served on, since small Austria, whose population amounted to less than a tenth of the Third Reich's population, was well known as a stronghold of fanatic Nazis. Austrians were quite well represented on the list of war criminals, starting with Hitler.

Cukurs' question made sense for another reason – I belonged to the age group that had been drafted to serve in the war.

'Yes,' I answered.

'Where, if I may ask?'

'On the Russian front,' I replied, and without thinking undid the buttons of my shirt and exposed a deep scar across my chest. The scar made a great impression on Cukurs. He must have thought that it was caused by a Bolshevik bullet that had penetrated my body in one of the battles on the eastern front when I, with my own hands, tried to block the spread of the loathed communism that had also been responsible for his having to flee his own homeland. It would have been interesting to see his reaction had he known that the scar was the result of a routine operation to remove an abscess I had undergone a few years back at Beilinson Hospital in Petah Tikvah, Israel. The sight of the scar made Cukurs try to establish the rapport of comrades-in-arm or male-bonding with the taciturn businessman who suddenly showed up in his life.

'And what rank did you hold in the army, if I may ask?'

I knew Cukurs served as a captain in the Latvian air force, and held a similar rank when serving with the Latvian

SS, and wondered whether I should mention a higher rank than his in order to impress him, or proceed with my minimalist approach and continue to foster the mystery that surrounded my character.

'Lieutenant,' I finally answered, and did not elaborate.

He did not believe me. My conduct was that of an educated man, someone of stature, and Cukurs, who was a great admirer of everything German, must have thought that I had served in the Wehrmacht in a much higher position, and that for personal reasons, probably because I didn't wish to draw too much attention to myself, had mentioned a relatively low rank.

Cukurs finally understood that he wouldn't elicit from me any detailed information about what had happened over 20 years ago, and let the conversation turn to tourism. Now it was my turn to pose questions.

Cukurs answered my questions at great length, and in detail, clearly making an effort to respond fully and correctly. Although nothing had been said, he started to think that perhaps I, Anton Kuenzle, businessman, was the embodiment of the unique opportunity, perhaps the last in his life, to considerably improve his standard of living. I had the feeling that Cukurs' head played host to some feverish ideas, namely that after all the long and trying years of living on the verge of poverty, perhaps through me he could succeed in once again becoming a respectable man, a man of means, with a position in society, just like that glorious period, those wonderful days in 1941.

Our conversation in the cabin lasted for almost an hour. In the meantime, business around the dock increased.

'I don't want to disturb you anymore. I can see you have a lot of work to do,' I said to Cukurs who, despite his interest in our chat was beginning to show signs of impatience.

'But Herr Kuenzle, it would be really nice if we could continue to discuss our common interests after work. I live in the Riviera quarter, not far from here, on the opposite bank. I'd be glad if you could come over, meet my family. Unfortunately though, it's a bit awkward on weekends, because of work. It's better we set a day during the week.'

Slowly, slowly, I told myself. No need to pay him a visit so soon. Let him stew for a while. Let him mull over the chance of joining the tourist venture of Anton Kuenzle and associates. Let him think of money until he cannot sleep. Let him think of gold and other shiny things. Outwardly I remained the cold and reserved businessman.

'I'm afraid this week is out of the question,' I answered matter-of-factly. 'I must go to Brasilia and Bahia. On business. I think I'll return to São Paulo next week sometime. If I have time, I'll get in touch with you.'

'I hope we'll meet again,' he said in a voice that betrayed his eagerness. 'I still have so many things to tell you, and I could show you a few interesting locations.'

We parted with a handshake.

That same evening a detailed report left São Paulo on its way to Europe. 'Made contact with The Deceased,' it said. 'The Deceased swallowed the bait. Seems I've been successful in gaining his confidence. I carry on. Anton.'

7
EXCURSIONS AND UNEXPECTED ENCOUNTERS

'IN 1956, shortly after he was sworn in, the President of Brazil, Joselino Kubitschek, decided to move the capital from Rio de Janeiro to the centre of the country,' I read in my tourist guide. 'Kubitschek wished to immortalize his presidency with a memorable public project. He announced, therefore, that he would realize, and immediately at that, the legislative proposal of 1891 decreeing that the capital of a vast state like Brazil, whose size is four times that of the European continent, should be in the centre of the country and not on the relatively crowded coast.'

I took another sip of the chilled juice cocktail the stewardess had brought me, and continued to read about the history of Brazil, on my flight from São Paulo to Brasilia. 'Kubitschek succeeded in enlisting the support of both houses of representatives, which, through an accelerated procedure, passed a resolution that allowed for the immediate start of planning and construction. Lucio Costa, the father of Brazil's modern architecture, together with his world-renowned colleague, Oscar Niemeyer, a personal friend of President Kubitschek, planned the city. And before the ink on their plans had dried, thousands of workers equipped with tractors and other modern equipment charged the barren land of the plateau, approximately 900 kilometres west of Rio. Four years later the government was already settled in the new town, Brasilia.'

'Beautiful country,' I said to my neighbour, a dapper man in his fifties. 'This is my first visit to Brazil, and I can't wait to see the famous architecture of the new capital.'

'It's definitely a unique place, beautiful and modern. A proof of what modern Brazil is capable of. Personally, though, I prefer lively Rio to Brasilia. As do most of my colleagues,' he responded in fluent English.

'Do you know Brasilia?' I asked.

'Yes, you could say that,' he replied, and smiled cheekily.

'My name is Kuenzle. I'm here on a business trip,' I introduced myself.

'Pleased to meet you. My name is Nicolão Tuma, and I'm a member of congress for the state of Acre.' He proceeded to explain that Acre lay in western Brazil, deep in the heart of the Amazon jungle, thousands of kilometres from the ocean, Rio and Brasilia.

Luck is working overtime, I thought to myself with satisfaction. I travel to Brasilia in order to foster the identity of Anton Kuenzle as a tourist and businessman, and who should I become acquainted with along the way but a member of congress. Not bad at all. Tuma turned out to be quite jovial, a lover of conversation and ready to help. 'Listen, when you get to Brasilia, you must go to Hotel Nacional. It's the most modern hotel in town. Speak to the hotel manager, tell him you're my friend, and you'll be treated very well.'

I tried to manipulate him into giving me his business card, reckoning that such a card could become helpful along the way. But Tuma turned out to be a seasoned politician, the kind that knows better than freely to hand out business cards, for fear that one day they might turn up in some dark corner and under odd circumstances, and cause him unnecessary embarrassment. In short, he would not give me his card, and I had to make do with writing down his address and telephone number in my small notebook.

From the oval window of the plane I could detect the outlines of the city as Costa and Niemeyer had planned it. It was made of two major crossed axes. From my bird's-eye view it looked like a gigantic airplane. Along the east–west axis stood public buildings, with the central train and bus station, hotels and stadium to the west, and to the east the cathedral, the national theatre and the government buildings, with their eye-catching twin towers.

As the plane came close to landing, Brasilia looked like a huge construction site, and actually a rather neglected one at that. Although formally it had already usurped Rio de Janeiro as the capital, Brasilia was still far from completion.

'No money,' explained my new friend Tuma, before we went our separate ways. 'The money is all gone. Kubitschek started building before there was even a road connecting the place to the rest of the world. All the building materials had to be flown in, and you can imagine how much that costs. Just think about it, every brick was brought here by "airmail"... In fact, our visionary president managed to impoverish Brazil and bring it to the verge of national bankruptcy. Now there is no money left for either building roads and apartment blocks, or laying down the infrastructure, not even to complete the work in those buildings that are already built. Apart from that, I wish you a pleasant stay in town.'

Tuma had a chauffeur-driven official car waiting for him. He waved goodbye to me, and disappeared inside it. I took a taxi to Hotel Nacional. The hotel seemed pleasant enough, but mentioning Tuma's name to the manager did not award the new guest any discount. Still, an efficient and pampering service was extended in the shape of colourful and tasty fruit baskets that kept appearing in my room. I quickly settled in, and went out to explore Brasilia.

My first tour of the new capital started off on the wrong foot. The nightmare for anybody working undercover with an assumed identity is to run into someone from their real life, in my case someone who knew me as Yitzhak, not as Anton Kuenzle. And this is exactly what happened to me at the entrance to the hotel. There I was, waiting for the tour bus, when suddenly I recognized a familiar figure just a few metres away – Joseph Nachmias, Israel's ambassador to Brazil, and formerly Israel's Commissioner of Police! This was all I needed – Israel's ambassador to Brazil approaching me, Anton Kuenzle, respectable Austrian businessman, just outside the lobby of the most luxurious hotel in Brasilia, calling out, 'Hi Yitzhak. What a surprise. How are things? What are you doing here? On your own, or is the wife with you?' And all of this in Hebrew! I took cover behind some columns until Nachmias went on his way to promote Israel's interests in Brazil's corridors of power. Fortunately, he left before the tour bus drew up in front of the hotel.

The tour of Brasilia was an experience. True, the momentum of construction had halted in many places, and the typical South American nonchalance was evident everywhere, but the tour made it clear why Niemeyer, who during the construction work had managed to edge out his colleague Costa and claim all the glory for himself, was considered such an architectural genius. Each building was outstanding, with its own unique character.

The Supreme Court had huge halls with inverted arches and a modern statue of Justice with eyes bound, directly facing the justices' chambers. The presidential building stood on marble columns and looked as if it were floating in the air. The cone-shaped cathedral towered 86 metres high from a base with a diameter of 60 metres, and had glass walls. Although its exterior did not look that impressive, its interior was amazing in its size.

It appeared that Kubitschek was particularly fond of diplomats, as the foreign ministry was rich with artificial waterfalls, fountains and pools. The elegant offices for Brazil's members of congress were placed in the twin towers, two high-rise buildings. At the time, the elected parliamentarians had little say in matters of state. The military, which had assumed power, was busy trying to stabilize the country's economy, and preferred to do it, for the time being, through shortened procedures, not always democratic, and in particular without the involvement of the members of congress. The two gigantic bowls, one convex, the other concave, which have since become the trademark of the new town, hosted the house of representatives and the senate.

The interior of the house of representatives was a large hall, amazing in its architecture, and full of ornaments. I noticed that Niemeyer had locked up the elected representatives in a closed chamber, devoid of windows and doors, with the only entrance through the lower floor. It had the feeling of a submarine, floating on its own, whose only connection to reality, the outside world, was through the staircase and the elevator, serving as a periscope.

As I followed the hand of the tour guide pointing out some interesting detail on the ceiling, the corner of my eye suddenly caught a familiar figure. No, it was not Ambassador Nachmias. Moreover, this time there were two familiar figures – Efrayim Ben-Artzi, director general of El-Al, and Shlomo Lahat, one of the directors of Israel's national airline.

This was too much, I thought to myself, as I tried to blend in better with my tour group. I had spent some months with Ben-Artzi in an officers' course of the Hagana, the Jewish defence organization of pre-state Israel, and I also knew Lahat quite well.

This unexpected encounter was the reason why I, after so many years of operational experience, still worked on a high state of alert, always anticipating the unexpected. Had anybody told me a few weeks back that one day in September I would be in Brazil hunting down a Nazi war criminal, and taking measures to avoid running into Efrayim Ben-Artzi and Shlomo Lahat in the chamber of the Brazilian Parliament, I would have responded, yes, everything's possible, and one must always be prepared for the most outlandish scenario. I spent the rest of the day with the pleasant tour through town, and kept a low profile in my tour group.

At night-time Brasilia became a ghost town, especially in comparison with lively Rio or São Paulo. It was easy to see why the congress members and top officials finished their work day in the early hours of the afternoon and rushed to the airport to catch one of the frequent flights out of dismal Brasilia to Rio de Janeiro or São Paulo. As yet unaware of this phenomenon, I spent the night in town, dining at the hotel restaurant, and the next morning took a flight back to the coast, this time to Bahia.

'These jungles never end,' I commented loudly, so that my neighbour could hear me. He was some years younger than me, around forty, and elegantly clad.

'You must be new here. We don't get excited at the sight anymore,' he responded, and introduced himself in perfect English, 'My name is Wilhelm Keller. I am the cultural attaché of the German embassy in Brasilia.'

We were soon conversing in German.

'Somewhere below us there is a very interesting project

going on,' Keller told me. 'We, the Germans, are sponsoring an experiment in which Israeli experts teach the local residents about modern agriculture and communal living. Something like the kibbutz. Have you ever heard about kibbutzim? Do you know what they are?' the German asked the Israeli who was impersonating an Austrian businessman.

'I have heard something about them,' I answered vaguely.

Thus, at an altitude of 20,000 feet above the Brazilian jungle, and over a light and delicious airline meal, I received a thorough lecture on the kibbutz from a young German diplomat. It was definitely one of those surreal situations that happen occasionally to those in our profession. I must give it to him, though – Herr Keller was indeed an expert on everything relating to the kibbutz movement, producing facts and figures, and quoting its history. I added his business card to the growing bundle in my bag.

Bahia welcomed us with a humid heat wave that hit us the minute we stepped out of the plane. As was my wont, soon after my arrival I found an organized tour through town, and booked myself on it. To my joy I discovered that this was the dead tourist season, and I was the only participant on this tour and consequently the sole centre of attention for the minibus driver and the tourist guide, a young female student who was quite knowledgeable about the place. She showed me all the wonders of Bahia, among them some of its 365 churches. In one of them, which also doubled as a museum, I noticed from afar my two friends from Brasilia, Efrayim Ben-Artzi and Shlomo Lahat. I wondered where else I was going to run into them as I ducked for cover. Fortunately though, our next meeting took place some time later in Tel-Aviv.

Bahia, its full name San Salvador de Bahia, was one of the most charming towns I had ever seen. The town is spread around a beautiful bay, the Bahia de Todos los Santos (Bay of All Saints), where the Europeans had landed in 1501. The first mission was led by Amerigo de Vespucci, after whom the entire continent was named. The entire region was bursting with green flora, particularly with palm trees. Brazil is blessed with approximately 600 different variety of this tree.

The natural bay made the town the centre of Portuguese rule, and for hundreds of years it served as the capital of Brazil. From here boatloads of gold, silver, precious stones, sugar and brazilwood set sail for Europe. This was where the European immigrants had landed, as well as the millions of slaves who had been kidnapped in Africa and shipped in cramped little boats to the new continent in order to work on the vast sugar plantations.

The centre of Bahia is crammed with palaces of all colours, built during the town's days of glory, which had remained in place when the town nearly came to a complete standstill when Rio became the new capital in 1763.

The percentage of Africans in Bahia, descendants of the slaves, is higher than the average in Brazil, a fact that lends the town its unique character. Even the food served in the many restaurants had a special aroma. Those in the know claim that the carnival of Bahia is livelier and more colourful than its tourist-oriented counterpart in Rio. The Bahianos foster the art of the *capoeira* – a mixture of dance and martial arts which employs mainly the legs. The dance requires great cooperation between the two dancers, since the slightest diversion from the prescribed movements and rhythm could end in a long and painful stay in hospital.

In the evening my tour guide took me to a local *macumba* ceremony, which in Bahia is called *candomble*. It was a mishmash of Christian and pagan rituals, filled with white and black gods, goddesses and saints. It also included the sacrifice of chickens, and was accompanied by loud, rhythmic music that hypnotized some and led others to hysteria. Many litres of *cachaca*, homemade sugar-cane based liquor, were imbibed by the participants. The *candomble* of Bahia was something completely different from the *macumba* ceremony I had seen in Rio on my second night in Brazil – it was unbelievably wild and authentic.

I used my days in Brasilia and Bahia to rest and gather my strength for what was to come next. Although almost two weeks had passed since I had left my home and family, I knew that despite my successes so far, the most difficult part lay still ahead of me.

8
TIGHTENING THE KNOT

BACK AT my hotel in São Paulo, several letters and telegrams awaited me. 'Requesting your authorization to close the US$100,000 deal we discussed prior to your departure,' said one of them. The others were in a similar vein, business deals that sprang out of Adi's imagination and were intended to foster my cover as a serious and important businessman, in whose diverse enterprises nothing moved without the personal authorization of the boss. I composed the appropriate responses, and rushed to the post office to send them.

'Sir, you'd better attach the stamps with extra glue,' advised the clerk and pointed to a small desk in the centre of the hall, on which a glass jar and tiny paintbrushes stood. 'A stamp that is not strongly glued on, double and triple, is bound to be peeled off the envelope by some postal worker who makes something extra on the side from selling second-hand stamps,' the clerk explained, both dispensing vital tourist information and providing a glimpse into survival tactics in Brazil's economy. I followed his advice, smeared a thick layer of glue on the back of the stamps, and sent the letters that also contained my reports.

Looking back, I sometimes find it difficult to believe that all my moves throughout this long and complicated operation were made without any forward-planning. I operated alone, thousands of kilometres from my home base, without back-up or direct means of communications. International telephone calls were then still a complicated undertaking. Not having anyone to talk to and consult with, I had to rely on my own wits and experience, initiate various steps, and act in accordance with developments. Consequently, following my instinct, I decided to use the following day, Friday, 25 September, to tighten my knot with The Deceased.

Almost one week had passed since our first meeting, at the end of which Cukurs had so warmly invited me to visit his home. I had no doubt that he was eager to see me again. After all, in his eyes I embodied the economic and social success he so longed for.

I tried to imagine what had gone through Cukurs' mind since our so-called accidental first encounter that had ended over a glass of brandy in the cabin of his rocking boat. It was clear that Herbert Cukurs missed his days of glory as deputy commander of the Riga ghetto. Then, he had been almost an almighty God, at least where the life and death of the Jews of Riga was concerned. He most probably recalled those days fondly when he was at the zenith of his power and glory, treated with great reverence and fear by anyone who saw him riding on horseback through the streets of the ghetto, clasping a heavy Nagan handgun, clad in his black leather pilot's coat. Then, he had unlimited power, the power to determine the fate of other people, and according to survivors' testimonies, he indeed exercised that power thousands, tens of thousands of times. He did it by sentencing those people to their death. Oh, how he must long for those days, which seem now, looking through the window of the shabby ticket office of his rundown boat-rental business, like a mirage produced by memory cells with an overdeveloped imagination.

Then one day, he accidentally, completely accidentally, meets a respectable Austrian businessman. Right from the start he manages to establish a rapport with the new acquaintance, not least due to their military service experiences, having fought on the same side in those 'good old days'. The Austrian seems as if he is trying to hide something, a man of few words, but from what little he does say, Cukurs understands that the new acquaintance presides over vast amounts of money, and that this Anton Kuenzle is looking for sound investment opportunities for his dollars and cruzeiros. And who knows, maybe with the help of Kuenzle and his backers' capital he will finally be able to pull himself out of this dismal existence, always on the verge of poverty, and become rich, a respectable member of society, and rid himself of the persecution of the Jewish organizations that have been beleaguering him for years. These were my musings as I drove from the centre of the city to the Riviera quarter. To my relief, locating the house was simple and easy. I parked the orange VW, and surveyed the surroundings.

At first glance it was evident that Cukurs took no chances. He lived in a compound that had been turned into a small fortress. It was surrounded by a high barbed-wire fence, and a large German shepherd guarded the iron-gated entrance, barking loudly and exposing its vicious fangs at the sight of the approaching stranger. The brick house itself was simple-looking and painted white. At the far end I noticed a tin-roofed shack that looked like a garden shed or a small workshop. The yard suffered from neglect, and was bereft of grass or flowers, with only a couple of trees that cast sparse shade.

'Good day. I'm looking for Herr Cukurs,' I said to the young man in front of the house, who must have been one of Cukurs' sons. He entered the house to report the visitor, and Cukurs emerged instantly. He grinned widely once his eyes succeeded in recognizing me through the thick lenses. He wore shabby, even tattered, work clothes.

'Herr Kuenzle! What a surprise. I'm so glad to see you.' Making sure that the leash of the scary and threatening guard dog was well tied to a metal pole, he walked quickly toward me.

The Deceased's handshake was as strong as at our first meeting, though a little longer, like good, old friends.

'Welcome. Please, come in,' he invited me, opening the front door.

During the years 1941–44 Cukurs had amassed a small fortune, robbed from his Jewish victims. But he had had to leave most of his loot in Latvia when he escaped the Red Army to the West, and the remains of the stolen goods had to be sold in order to finance the long escape route from Riga to São Paulo.

In the autumn of 1964, Cukurs' home showed no traces of the spoils of war. Simple furniture was scattered in the living room. The Cukurs family lived modestly, bordering on poverty, and yet their standard of living was much higher than that of the Eichmann family, who had lived in a tiny house, without electricity or running water, on Garibaldi Street in Buenos Aires.

From the kitchen emerged a woman in her fifties, thin, graceless, with unkempt hair.

'Guten Tag,' she said in German, shook my hand, and once more disappeared inside the kitchen.

In the hallway leading to the living room stood a medium-sized chest of drawers. Cukurs stopped by it, and pulled out from one of its drawers a large pile of decorations and medals.

Time to make an impression, I thought. He was certainly trying to impress me. There were some 15 decorations in the heap, representing well the political upheavals his homeland had gone through in the past decades. Cukurs was proud of each and every one of them. Gloating, he presented to me the Order of Santos Dumont medal, which he had received after his flight to Gambia – an acknowledgment of his contribution to the development of civil aviation. There was also a Russian medal he had received in 1940, when Latvia had been under Soviet rule and he had worked at the Yakovlev airplane plant, named after the inventor of the Yak planes. Despite his hatred of the Russians and everything they stood for, he was still proud of this medal. Most of the other decorations were German, and many of them bore the swastika. At that moment I preferred not to think of the activities for which Cukurs had been awarded these decorations.

'And look what I have here!' He opened another drawer and began to empty its contents. There was an entire arsenal there – a 7.65mm calibre FN handgun, a 6.35mm Beretta, a 7.63 automatic Mauser, and a 5.56 semi-automatic rifle. 'The Brazilian secret service gave me a licence for all these toys,' he said with pride. 'I want you to know that I know how to take good care of myself.'

Was this a warning? Or was this just another attempt to impress me, Anton Kuenzle, former German army officer who had been wounded in a heroic battle against the Bolsheviks on the Eastern Front?

1. Anton Kuenzle being filmed by Cukurs at their penultimate meeting in São Paulo.

2. Milda, Gunnar and Herbert Cukurs Junior point at Kuenzle's photograph distributed by Interpol, and claim: 'This man liquidated Cukurs.'

3. The Hangman of Riga, a few days before his fateful journey to Montevideo.

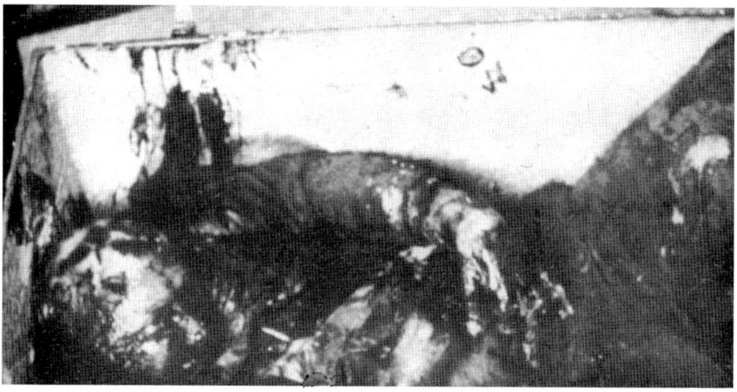

4. Cukurs' body as it was found by Uruguay's police.

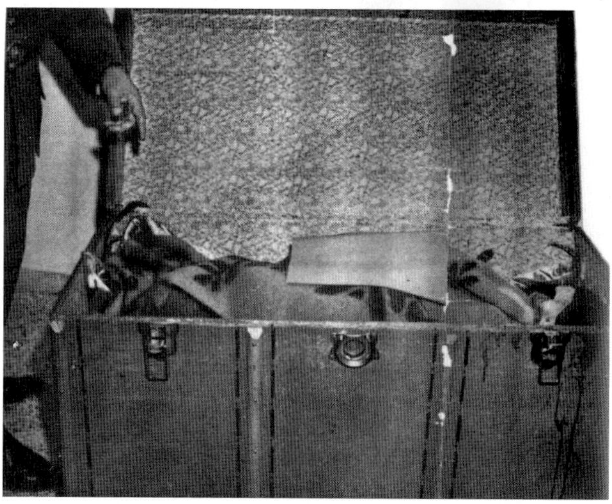

5. Cukurs' body wrapped in a blanket. On the body, the death sentence written on a sheet of paper.

6. Cukurs in Brazil, 1950.

7. The restaurant facing Cukurs' dock. Taken in 1995.

8. Cukurs in the cockpit of the small plane he had built and flown from Latvia to Gambia, which earned him the name of Latvia's Lindbergh.

9. Herbert and Milda Cukurs in Paris, 1945, on the escape route to Brazil.

10. Cukurs at a press conference at the end of the 1950s, in which he claimed his innocence.

11. Cukurs proudly displays his uniform from his heyday as the famous captain of Latvia's air force.

12. Cukurs and his Brazilian-born youngest son. He hoped to obtain Brazilian nationality through his son. Kuenzle believed it was his grandson.

13. Cukurs by his seaplane, in which he flew Kuenzle over São Paulo.

14. A Nazi German passport Cukurs obtained in Berlin, 1944, following his flight from Riga.

15. The only photo of Cukurs during the war.

16. Photographs of the massacre of Latvia's Jews in December 1941, taken by Carl Sturm, a member of the SS who participated in it.

It won't be easy to eliminate him, I thought as I made appropriate sounds of amazement at the sight of the weapon collection.

Cukurs used every means at his disposal to try and impress me. He took me on a guided tour, and showed me his workshop, in which he repaired boat engines. In the middle of the shack stood a very old Cadillac, which must have once been a great car, and was now in pieces.

'I'm almost finished working on it,' he said. 'Another push, a couple of investments, and the old lady's as good as new.'

He's just boasting, I thought. I didn't think this car would be driving the streets in the foreseeable future. On the other hand, if it were to happen, then this man had considerable technical talent.

'I have given some thought to our previous conversation, and I believe I can help you in finding interesting investment opportunities,' he said as he poured us a brandy in his rundown office in the shack. 'Here are some aerial photographs I have taken. I would have no problem taking more. After all, I fly over this area almost every day. I shall also be very glad to take you on a tour of the area in a car, so that you get to know it a little.'

I was pleased with my success. Cukurs had swallowed the bait hook, line and sinker, and was ready to do business. So let's hear what he has to say about the Interlagos area, I thought.

We spent the morning driving through the area. I was behind the wheel, and Cukurs was the tour guide. It was a crushingly boring tour.

He too must have sensed the boredom, and decided to try another tack. 'I have two large farms inland,' he said all of a sudden. 'They could be suitable for your investors. I'll be only too glad to show them to you.'

So now he was trying to present himself as a landowner. Then again, he might have some hidden treasures and choose not to display his wealth out of personal security considerations, I thought, and decided to check it further.

'So what do you say?' Cukurs continued. 'Want to see my plantations? We had better do it on a weekday, though.

Now I must take care of my business. The holiday makers are coming in droves.'

As was my wont, I put on the show of a very busy man trying to find a window in my calendar. We agreed on the middle of the following week.

'I'll try and fix the Cadillac by then, and we'll travel like kings,' he managed to say and returned to his work, not before promising to see me again in a few days.

Sure. If the Cadillac is repaired by then, I'm a beetle, I thought, and rubbed my poor back that would have to endure the long, slow and tiring trip in the VW. One thing was clear, though, I was going to wear boots on this journey, following Cukurs' advice, who warned me in his deep voice, 'You must be careful. The area there is swarming with many poisonous snakes.'

In order to learn more about snakes, I used one of my free days to visit the Butanta Institute, São Paulo's reptile research centre. The scientists of this world-renowned centre held more than 60,000 different varieties of poisonous snakes, scorpions and spiders. The main attraction of the place was the twice daily milking of the snakes' venom, performed in front of the visitors. The venom was then used to produce anti-venom. As I prepared for my trip with Cukurs, I felt I had earned the right to loosen up a little.

These were the glory days of Brazilian football, thanks to its star player, Pelé, and to two consecutive World Cup victories, against Sweden in 1958 and Czechoslovakia in 1962. The hotel reception clerk told me about an interesting forthcoming match at São Paulo stadium. A football match between the Santos and São Paulo teams. A match between these two was considered in Brazil to be almost a local contest, since Santos was the port town of São Paulo, and Pelé had been the Santos' star for many years. As a veteran football fan I decided to seize the opportunity and treat myself. On the way to the stadium, the heavens opened and a tropical downpour turned the streets into muddy canals. No chance they'd be playing in such weather, I thought to myself. After all, they're playing football, not water polo.

I turned around, and spent the rest of the day in the hotel. Only later did I find out how wrong I had been, thinking like a typical Mediterranean football fan. São Paulo's sewage system had indeed collapsed that day, but the drainage at the municipal stadium had been in much better shape. Bang on time, the referee had blown the whistle, and the game had kicked off. And I had missed it!

9
CONFRONTATION IN THE JUNGLE

THE ROAD from São Paulo to Cukurs' plantation was dull. The vast monotonous plain passed by the Beetle's windows. Of course the Cadillac had not been ready. I drove, Cukurs navigated, and we were mostly silent, which suited me fine.

He addressed me as Herr Kuenzle, whereas I called him by his first name, Herbert. Anyone familiar with the etiquette of spoken German could discern that I was boss in the small car.

It was Tuesday, 29 September 1964. Only 17 days had passed since I had emerged from the Air France Boeing in Rio de Janeiro. All in all, I should have been more than pleased with my achievements so far. In the preliminary war of wits between us, I had a definite advantage. Herbert Cukurs, the Hangman of Riga, was travelling with me, in my car, on the way to one of his plantations, desperately trying to win over my heart and wallet. But my work had taught me that even an experienced man like myself could be mistaken. A journey like this, to a remote place, could also prove to be dangerous. Perhaps this was a sophisticated trap laid for me?

I was bothered by these thoughts, and so before picking up Cukurs from his home I had stopped at a small sporting goods shop and purchased a pocketknife. It was a plain pocketknife, not some combat weapon; a pocketknife with a blade long and sharp enough in case it transpired that the ever-suspicious Cukurs was also an excellent actor and, having somehow uncovered my identity and intentions, was now leading me to some remote place in the jungle to settle his account with me. I knew that he was armed with one of his handguns, and on the road he told me that he had also brought along a semi-automatic rifle. I realized that my new purchase, the small pocketknife, was no match in this arms race, but having it in my pocket, I at least did not feel utterly defenceless.

On the way to Piedade, a small town near one of his plantations, Cukurs told me that his manager there was a *pistolero* and a former bodyguard of President Kubitschek's. Was this another of his attempts to let me know that he was always cautious and on guard, or was he simply bragging, trying to show off his connections to people in high places? To this day, I have no idea.

I was not really worried, and definitely not scared, but I was prepared for all eventualities. I even had ready a credible cover story for our joint pee-breaks. Yes, this constituted a problem to an Israeli Jew who came to South America to hunt down a Nazi and found himself peeing with him on some remote roadside. What would I do if he discovered that I was circumcised? I had prepared a reasonable cover story, with an acceptable plot for a man like Cukurs. If he had asked, I was going to tell him that during the war I had contracted gonorrhoea on a visit to a military brothel on the Russian front, and remind him that in the days before antibiotics the treatment of this sexually transmitted disease included, in some cases, the removal of the foreskin. But he never asked. Perhaps because he was so self-absorbed during our roadside stops, being at the advanced age of 64, when the bladder takes centre stage in the daily lives of many men.

Rancho Corujas, Cukurs' first farm, which we reached at midday, appeared to be a small, rundown plantation. Cukurs took to heart my unenthusiastic reaction to the sight, and hastened to tell me that the second farm, Rancho Esclavados, was 'much more interesting'.

We arrived there in the late afternoon.

'I have 120,000 banana trees here,' Cukurs said with pride, as the VW skipped and hopped along the dirt road leading to the place. 'It's four kilometres long,' he informed me.

True, I did not expect to see Dallas' Ewing family's Southfork ranch house, but Cukurs' Rancho Esclavados, if it was indeed his, did not look like a prosperous agricultural enterprise, to say the least. The place was, indeed, crammed with banana trees, but except for the small wooden shack and tiny corrugated-iron storeroom standing in a dusty clearing, there was nothing hinting at success. It should be noted, however, that despite the poor-looking structures, the groves where the thousands of well-tended banana trees grew looked neat, orderly and clean. The place was deserted. There was no sign of Kubitschek's *pistolero*, or anybody else for that matter.

A trap?

Later developments definitely suggested such a possibility.

'Let's take a short walk,' my host suggested, and pointed to a small path leading to an uncultivated area full of trees and tall bushes. 'It leads to a small river swarming with crocodiles.'

I knew that Cukurs was observing my reactions closely, and hastened to accept his offer without any hesitation.

Cukurs carried a waterproof bag along. He halted after a few hundred metres, before reaching the thicket, opened the bag, and produced his semi-automatic rifle.

The pocketknife isn't going to be much help here, I thought and wondered what would happen next.

'I'm sure you still remember something of your glorious past on the eastern front,' he said. 'Let's have a shooting match. See the target hanging there, on that tree?' He pointed at a tin plate hanging about 50 metres away.

I had no doubt in my mind that this shooting competition was no spur-of-the-moment idea. It was a well-planned move by Cukurs, intended to put me to the test, and maybe even beyond it.

'With pleasure,' I responded.

Cukurs loaded the rifle with ten rounds, took aim, and started shooting. He shot fast, with the expertise that comes from experience, a large part of which had been acquired by shooting naked and petrified Jews in the head in the Valley of the Dead in Rombula Forest, where thousands had been murdered in the winter of 1941.

Cukurs' ten shots were grouped within a 5-centimetre radius – a decent result.

'Your turn,' he said proudly, handing me the rifle.

After all, I had told him that I had been an officer in the Nazi army, and now I could see out of the corner of my eye how he followed my every move, waiting to find out whether I was an impostor or really had a rich, military past.

There was no fear in me, nor did I shake. From the minute I had taken this mission upon myself, Anton Kuenzle had become an inseparable part of me. According to the cover story, Kuenzle had served in the Nazi army on the eastern front. I, on the other hand, had worn King George the Sixth's uniform for six years, and then served a good few years as an officer in the IDF, where I had risen to a senior rank. I was not lacking in military experience.

I squeezed the trigger with an expertise and speed that surpassed that of Cukurs. Had my past shooting instructors seen the grouping I made in the centre of the target, they would have applauded me: a 3-centimetre radius.

'Way to go, Herr Anton!' Cukurs called out loudly, and added an amiable slap on my shoulder. I noticed that he addressed me as Herr Anton instead of Herr Kuenzle. The shooting match, as it transpired, penetrated yet another wall of suspicion Cukurs had surrounded himself with during his 20 years on the run. Now he was almost completely convinced that I was all right.

As of that moment, the atmosphere between us became much lighter. As if the shooting match was some male ritual intended to transform the blood fraternity of the two former comrades-in-arms in the service of the Führer into a brotherhood. We were, he was beginning to believe, not just comrades-in-arms but also in fate.

We walked on along the path, when suddenly I felt a sharp pain in my foot. An errant nail had pierced the sole of my boot and stuck hard in my foot. I sat on the ground, took off my boot, and examined the damage. It was a light wound.

'Here, take my gun, and knock down the bastard nail's head,' Cukurs suggested amiably and, holding the barrel, handed me the gun. The magazine was in, the gun was loaded.

One bullet in the head at point-blank range, another bullet in the heart to ascertain death, and the mission is complete, I thought. By the time they find him here, in this remote corner of the world, I shall be long gone to Europe.

'Thanks. Great idea,' I said, took the gun from Cukurs, and with a few well-aimed butt blows, hammered the nail back into place.

We crossed over the crocodile river on a wobbly, wooden bridge. I noticed the silhouette of at least one crocodile in the water, which justified the name Cukurs gave his river. When the sun began to set, we returned to the shack.

Darkness engulfed us suddenly, without twilight, as happens in this part of the world. The pale light of the small paraffin lamp attracted myriad flies, mosquitoes and fleas to us. Driven by their interest in variety and the new taste, the insects preferred to assault me.

We settled on folding wooden chairs outside the small shack. Cukurs prepared a makeshift dinner. He opened a few cans, produced cheese and salami from his waterproof bag, and cut a loaf of black bread into thick slices. We hardly spoke, preferring to listen to the voices of nature and to sink into our own private thoughts.

I could not help but think of my family, exterminated in the Holocaust by murderers similar to the man who sat less than a metre away from me. I was the only son of a well-off family, and had a fairly uneventful childhood. My grandfather had served as a sergeant major in the Prussian army in 1870, during the Prussian–French war. My mother was a German, English and Latin teacher. My father was a respectable ear-nose-and-throat doctor, whose fame had reached beyond the boundaries of our town. He was not only a proud Jew, but also a German patriot, who wore with pride the Iron Cross he had been awarded for valour in the bitter battles on the western front, in Mars-la-Tour near Verdun, during the early days of the First World War.

We had lived in a respectable house in the centre of the town, overlooking the pretty square. The municipal theatre lay just across the square, and my parents were invited to every new show since my father served as the theatre doctor, and took good care of the hoarse throats and vocal cords that failed their owners minutes before curtain call.

The Germany of my childhood and youth was a torn country in perpetual crisis. The defeat in the First World War, the Treaty of Versailles, which the German public perceived as a humiliation, the terrible economic crisis of the 1920s with its galloping inflation that wiped clean all the savings of the middle classes – all of these tore the German nation apart.

The balcony of our home had provided me with a unique vantage point on the political life of Germany at large, and our town in particular. Every few days one or another demonstration took place. Once it was the communists, then the socialists, or the Nazis, or the conservatives. As a child I had witnessed how the Left – the communists and socialists in all their various factions – wasted its strength in bloody, internal fighting, and thus paved the way for the Nazis, who came to power in 1933.

I was a student at the high school for the humanities, the Johannes Gymnasium, where many of the teachers and students were Jews. My homeroom teacher, whom I had considered a great humanist, appeared with the swastika on his lapel one day after Hitler was elected chancellor of Germany. And he was not the only one. Incidentally, after the war I read a study that attempted to explain the phenomenal success the Nazi movement had among German teachers. It appears that Hitler's writings, which included weighty chapters on the reorganization of the Germanic nation and placed great emphasis on order and nearly blind obedience, held considerable appeal for the teachers.

Within no time at all, we, the Jews, became the target of persecution and harassment. Each class now started with standing to attention and raising the right arm in the 'Heil Hitler' salute. We, the Jewish students, were exempt from the salute, but not from standing stiff and upright in honour of the Führer. Instead of biology, we now had to study race theory, which included, among other things, detailed explanations of the alleged danger to the German nation from the 100,000 Ostjuden – Jewish émigrés from eastern Europe who lived in the Reich and were taking over Germany's economy and cultural life. No one spoke yet of the annihilation of the Jews, but the persecution and restrictions had become a day-to-day reality. Anti-Jewish slogans, boycotts of Jewish shops and businesses, travel restrictions, confiscation of finances; and then there were the testimonies regarding the deportation of Jews to concentration camps. One by one, my father's patients disappeared. The authorities insisted that another specialist, a non-Jew, treat their Aryan ear-nose-and-throat ailments.

'I can't stand it anymore,' I had told my parents one day. It was in 1934. I had been an active member of the Zionist youth movement 'Habonim', and decided that the time had come for me to fulfil the Zionist dream.

Unlike most German Jewish youths who emigrated to Palestine during that period, I had decided that the kibbutz, with all due respect to the pioneers, was not the ideal place for me. The idea of communal life did not appeal to me. I was looking for an alternative.

In 1934, the Nazis still allowed Jews who had managed to obtain an entry visa to any country in the world to leave Germany. My parents considered themselves too old and settled to abandon the country they saw as their homeland. It is worth mentioning that my father was no businessman and did not have much money readily available, not the amount that could have afforded him to start a new life. But my parents had some connections which helped them contact Dr Biram, the principle of the Hebrew Reali High School in Haifa, Palestine. They asked him to accept me as a student in his school.

After examining my school records, Dr Biram agreed, and I received the so longed-for certificate that allowed me to immigrate to the Land of Israel.

In October 1934 I left my family and Germany. Among the many documents I packed were my outstanding sportsman award stamped with a large swastika, from the Reich's youth olympics of 1933, and my report card with an exceptionally high grade in mathematics. I deserved this high grade, but the fact that it was put on my report card at all was thanks to my maths teacher, a dear man, who felt genuinely sorry about my departure. His insistence on writing my grade on the report card was his way of expressing his disgust with the Nazi regime. Before I left, he even shook my hand and wished me the best of luck on my new path.

I remember to this day the moments of departure from my family and hometown. The whistle of the train as it slowly rolled out of the main train station adorned with dozens of huge Nazi flags still rings in my ears. My parents stood on the platform and waved goodbye to their 15-year-old son, travelling on his own to a far-off land. At that moment I felt I was cutting myself off from everything German, preparing to become a proud Jew in the Land of Israel.

My life in Haifa was difficult at the beginning. Coming from the high school for the humanities in Germany, I landed in the high school for the sciences in Palestine, in which even mathematics and physics were taught in Hebrew, never mind the Bible lessons, of which I understood nothing in the first days. But I adapted very quickly to my new surroundings, and being good at sports, I soon acquired new friends, among them Chaim Laskov, who later became the Israeli army's fifth chief of staff. He became my 'welfare officer', and greatly helped my integration into this new society.

Twice I returned to Germany for family visits, the last time being in the summer of 1936. The Nazis had then hosted the Olympics Games in Berlin, and were trying to present to the world a respectable and cultured façade. The poisonous anti-Semitic posters had been removed, at least for a couple of weeks. But from the stories of my friends, I managed to form a realistic picture of the situation. I understood that the Jews in Germany were suffering, but I could not have fathomed that they were facing annihilation. This was simply inconceivable in the land that had given Beethoven, Goethe and Schiller to the world.

I saw my father one last time, in the summer of 1937. The Nazis allowed my parents to travel to Hungary, where we met at a holiday resort. In the summer of 1938, he was not allowed to leave the country, but my mother managed to obtain a visitor's permit to Yugoslavia, and we spent time together at the holiday resort town of Bled, near a lake, in Slovenia. By then I had already completed my high-school studies with great success, had become a citizen of

Palestine, and had joined the Hagana, the underground defence organization in pre-state Israel was established. After spending two weeks together, I said goodbye to my mother, not knowing that this was the last time I would ever see her.

We wrote letters to each other right up to the start of the Second World War, but when the fighting began, our contact was broken. In September 1939, in the first week of the war, I enlisted in the Royal Artillery of the British army, the first volunteer in Palestine to His Majesty's loyal forces.

During the war I received the occasional Red Cross postcard from Germany, bearing brief regards from my parents. The last postcard was sent in June 1943. 'Regards from Aunt Theresa', it said, but I had no aunt by such a name. By that time, rumours about the Theresienstadt concentration camp had already reached Palestine, and my parents had indeed been deported there in June 1943, on the last transport out of Germany. Theresienstadt was designated as the concentration camp for famous or privileged people. My parents were sent there because of the Iron Cross my father had been awarded for valour and his readiness to sacrifice his life for kaiser and country, the country that then sent him to his death.

From testimonies I gathered after the war, I learned that my father died in Theresienstadt in May 1944. A short while afterwards, my mother was transported to Auschwitz where, together with millions of other Jews, she was murdered by the Nazis, who were assisted by monsters like Cukurs.

'I suggest we go to sleep,' the Latvian voice broke into my stream of memories.

We spent the night in the small shack. There were two metal-framed beds along one wall, head to head, on which we spread our sleeping bags. I noticed Cukurs hiding his handgun under the pillow, although there was nobody else in the vicinity apart from me.

Twenty years on the run leave their impact on a man, I thought before falling asleep.

Despite the oppressing presence of Cukurs and the mosquitoes, I slept well on the whole, and from my wife's reports I knew that my sleep was very light and that I did not talk in my sleep; at the most, I grind my teeth. But grinding teeth could hardly expose me to Cukurs as an Israeli whose only wish was to help end his life, and the sooner the better. In the middle of the night I woke to a sudden noise coming from Cukurs' bed. Despite the darkness I managed to discern Cukurs rising from his bed. He pulled the gun from under his pillow, stuck it in his pyjama bottoms, and left the shack.

My heart started to race. What was he doing? What was he up to? To be on the safe side, I grabbed my personal weapon, the poor, small pocketknife I had purchased in São Paulo.

The sound of water spurting against a small tree clarified the picture – theatre of the absurd. A hunted Nazi war criminal was standing in the middle of the Brazilian forest, a loaded gun for defence against unidentified enemies stuck in the elastic of his pyjama bottoms, and peeing against a small tree.

Killing him won't be easy, I thought in German, before falling back to sleep. The Deceased continues to be watchful and cautious, and this must be emphasized in all of my reports.

10
COFFEE AND CAKE IN THE MONSTER'S HOME

THE REPORT I sent to Europe detailed all the steps I had taken so far. I also gave a broad account of our trip inland, to Cukurs' plantations, and explained that I was trying gradually to accustom The Deceased to the ever-growing distances of our joint journeys, so that leaving Brazil would eventually seem quite natural to him.

I knew that the elimination would have to take place outside Brazil, not least in order to spare Brazilian Jews from Nazi retaliation. But how should it be done? What would be the safest way? A bullet from afar? Perhaps poisoning? Maybe a point-blank shot in the back of the head?

In all my reports I reiterated and stressed the fact that despite The Deceased's age of 64, he was still a dangerous man, alert, physically strong and resourceful. At the time my friends thought that I was exaggerating the danger. But at the end of the operation it was Yoav who admitted in front of all the participants, 'And it transpired that Yitzhak's warnings were indeed accurate all along.'

But this was still far off, and in the meantime it was true that Cukurs had swallowed the bait, but he still swam in deep waters and as long as he did, the battle was far from over. I kept reeling in, then releasing the line, only to reel in again, and then let go. I feared that I would have to repeat this act many more times. Our journey to the farms proved to be quite significant in terms of our relationship. Cukurs had become almost entirely convinced – his innate suspicion would not allow him to become fully so – that the Austrian businessman, Anton Kuenzle, was considering him as a potential partner. Thus, a few days later, Cukurs suggested of his own accord that we visit nearby Santos and check out the holiday resorts there.

'Excellent idea!' I seized the opportunity. 'I suggest we also check out the holiday-homes market. What the terms of rent are, what kind of deposit is asked for, what the minimum rental period is, and so on.'

Cukurs consented immediately, of course, and my request that he accompany me on a tour of houses I had already seen seemed to him quite natural. I wanted to get him used to entering vacant houses without a second thought, especially not the thought that someone was waiting for him inside with a loaded gun. My new interest in holiday homes was meant to do just that.

In the course of our search for suitable investment locations, we spent a pleasant, quiet day in Santos. We visited houses along the shore of the town, at the Praia Grande. It is difficult to describe Brazil's long beaches. It is simply another world. During my trips with Cukurs, it dawned on me that it was just a question of time before Brazil, a beautiful country with a fascinating, varied population, became a magnet for tourists from all over the world.

On the way back from Santos to São Paulo, Cukurs took the initiative again. 'We should take a look at what's happening in Porto Alegre,' he suddenly suggested, which pleased me no end because it fitted in perfectly with my plans. Porto Alegre was the ideal place – a coastal town, hundreds of kilometres south of São Paulo, and not too far from the border with Uruguay.

'What a great idea,' I responded with enthusiasm. 'You have no idea how glad I am we met. It must have been fate that brought us together. You are at home here, you know the South American mentality, command the language, and know how to do business here. This is great. Just great. I invite you to fly with me to Porto Alegre, all expenses – flight, hotel, food – on me. However,' I remembered the old Arab proverb 'Haste is from the devil,' and added, 'I'm quite busy this week. Let's go next Monday.'

The invitation made Cukurs happy. As far as he was concerned, this was another small step towards economic independence. But in the meantime he still had to return to his dismal reality full of hundreds of bothersome weekend vacationers wanting to rent a boat for a couple of hours. I drove him home and we said goodbye, with me promising we'd meet again in Porto Alegre.

I arranged my schedule for the next few days so that I could pay a visit to the Iguacu Falls, one of the most breathtakingly beautiful natural spots in the world, and from there take the most reasonable route to Porto Alegre.

Anyone who wishes to receive confirmation of the old cliché about man's insignificance in comparison with the might of nature should visit the Iguacu Falls. The waterfalls, and there are several of them, are at the point where two rivers, the Rio Parana and Rio Iguacu, converge, near the triangular borders of Brazil, Argentina and Paraguay. Although most of the falls are on Argentinean territory, the best vantage point is on the Brazilian side. To reach this point one has to walk a long and winding path through thick, green foliage leading directly to the heart of the falls. The noise is deafening. The air is misty, filled with water drops. In the local Indian dialect, Iguacu means 'storming waters'. Seventeen-hundred cubic metres per second of falling waters along a stretch of four kilometres! Only a few minutes of this could have fulfilled half the State of Israel's annual water requirement.

According to my plan, we made our way to Porto Alegre separately. Cukurs arrived from São Paulo on a commercial flight, and went straight to the Everest Palace Hotel, where I had booked rooms for us. In order to make him feel secure, I arranged for him to get there first.

I landed in Porto Alegre a few hours later. After arriving at the hotel, I went to look for him in his room. Some seconds passed following my knock on the door. Suddenly it was pulled ajar to reveal Cukurs standing, a gun in his hand.

The snake is always on his toes, I thought. I pointed at the gun, and said half-jokingly, 'So what is it, Herbert? Scared of me?'

'If you had a long nose, then I would've had good reason to be scared. Anyway, one must always be on the alert,' he said, and returned the gun to his pocket.

Cukurs was not joking. It was no accident that he had mentioned a long nose, which according to the Nazis was a Jewish characteristic. He meant every word he said. He was serious, deadly serious.

'Let's take a look at the town,' I suggested, and Cukurs agreed immediately.

If there is one thing I cannot stand, it's hypocrisy, and Cukurs was a natural-born hypocrite. He tried to please me at all costs, and consequently made an effort to adjust his behaviour to mine. It drove me mad! But Cukurs also had his positive sides, which actually made life easier for me. Earlier on in our acquaintance he had already noticed that I was the silent type. He therefore kept to himself, and refrained from making small-talk, which was just fine, since I had no interest whatever in either soul-searching conversations or superficial chitchat. We did not speak of politics, nor pass comments about women, and did not mention the old Germany, not even the Nazis. Only once, during the course of a routine conversation, he suddenly mentioned Oberstrumbannführer Josef Kramer, the commander of the Bergen-Belsen concentration camp. I assumed that it was yet another attempt to put me to the test. Otherwise our conversations revolved mostly around investments and tourism. I took great care to circumvent the issue of our financial relations, or mention it only in the vaguest of terms.

I had no interest in buying him, but I did want to give him the feeling that a relationship was slowly forming between us, in which he played a vital role, albeit not a clearly defined one. I covered all of our expenses, of course, and seized every opportunity to demonstrate that money was no object for me and my business associates. I made sure to get the bill for all our meals, and spoke of future investments, which, to realize, I would need his good services.

Cukurs tried to maintain a semblance of reciprocity, and would occasionally buy us a cup of coffee. More than that he could not afford.

One night, at the end of a sumptuous dinner – the sign of the good life Cukurs so longed for and had not enjoyed ever since his days of glory in Nazi-occupied Latvia – in the course of a conversation about business trips, I managed to get him interested in travelling abroad. All of a sudden he was wondering aloud about getting an alien's passport. Cukurs could not hold a regular Brazilian passport since pressure from Jewish organizations had prevented him from obtaining Brazilian citizenship, and he would now need an alien's passport in order to accompany me on my business trips to neighbouring countries.

'Is it difficult to get one?' I asked flatly, concealing my true feelings.

'No, Not at all. It's just a question of paying a middleman a modest sum. US$30 or so.'

'No problem, then.' I raised my glass to him. 'It's on me. After all, it's me who needs a local partner like yourself. As for the gun,' I added with a smile, 'you have nothing to worry about. I'll get it through the border controls for you.'

Cukurs grinned back. Most of the time he kept a poker face, not disclosing his emotions. But this time there were laughter lines around his eyes, which sparkled with genuine joy over what seemed to him as a significant development on his way to happiness and wealth. His greed did not subside even when the head of the security services in São Paulo, who were responsible for his security, and to whom he turned for advice, warned Cukurs against leaving the country.

'It's safe to assume that your enemies haven't forgotten you. I can protect you here, in São Paulo, but my jurisdiction stops at the border,' recalled Señor Alcido Cintra Bueno Filho some months later, reconstructing the conversation in which he had tried to persuade Cukurs to stay in São Paulo.

'I trust the man,' had been Cukurs assured reply. 'And anyway, I've never been a coward.' Not only that, but Cukurs was also a man of great self-control, as I found out a few days later. I invited him to dinner at the fancy restaurant Chalet Swiss, on the 25th floor of the hotel I was staying in.

'Let's go to a nightclub, have some fun,' I suggested at the end of our meal. We went to a reputable Japanese nightclub. São Paulo had a large community of Japanese immigrants at the time. Cukurs noted with pleasure the way the maître d' welcomed me, his newfound friend, the man of the world, with great warmth, as if we had been old friends. Little did he know that only a few days earlier I had frequented this establishment, and, with the help of handsome tips, had made my rounded self memorable in the mind's of everyone who worked there, precisely in order to impress Cukurs right at the entrance.

The maître d' showed us the way to a good table, from where we had a perfect view of the floor show. Two pretty hostesses tried to join us, but our cold responses sent them on their way again.

'So, what do you drink in São Paulo?' I asked my guest, who made no attempt to conceal his joy at the treat.

'Cuba libre,' he said, 'rum and coke.'

I had expected an evening of heavy drinking and so, before leaving the hotel, I had swallowed two spoonfuls of butter, an old and still-effective trick, in which the butter lines the stomach and slows down the alcohol absorption into the bloodstream.

'*Prosit!*' I raised my Cuba libre, hoping many more would follow.

'*Prosit*,' he echoed.

Some young women performed a local and not particularly successful version of the cancan on the dance floor, while we again discussed the tourism business. Despite the easy, relaxed atmosphere, Cukurs declined to imbibe uncontrollably. I noticed he drank very slowly; he would start with a small sip, as if examining the contents of the glass, then wait a few minutes, and only then start drinking. He behaved like someone afraid of being poisoned, I noted, and realized that poisoning was out of the question. Having emptied his first glass, he allowed the waiter to refill it once, but no more. Two glasses was all he had, and they left no visible impression on him. He never lets go, not even when he had a good time with a man who had already undergone numerous tests, I concluded. No matter what, he always stays fully alert, always ready to fight back.

And yet, something in Cukurs' attitude toward me had changed after all.

'I got my passport, and my visa to Uruguay,' he said one day. 'We can take our trip there as planned. I would really like it if you came and visited me and my family first,' he offered, proud of his achievements, and of the opportunity to be the host for once. And so I found myself one afternoon in the Cukurs' family living room, among the entire family – father, mother, the three sons and daughter-in-law – sipping coffee and eating a Viennese apple strudel.

Having coffee at the Cukurs' fortress was completely surreal. Due to his mistrust, strangers rarely visited the Cukurs' residence, definitely not to drink coffee and eat cake. And I, the guest, became a real attraction for the rest of the family, who must have forgotten when the last time was that a stranger sat in their living room.

They weighed every sentence I said, and closely examined every move I made. Cukurs and his wife spoke reasonable German, and their Dresden-born daughter-in-law, whose heart I had won on the way to my first meeting with The Deceased, occasionally translated choice parts of our conversation to the rest of the family. Of course I complimented the apple strudel Milda Cukurs had baked especially for me, and it was no lie – the cake was definitely tasty.

I let Cukurs and his family take over the conversation. They were very polite, as Europeans can be, so much so that they refrained from asking personal questions, which suited me.

'I must take one more short trip to Uruguay, and then I'm flying back to Europe,' I told my hosts. 'I'm going to propose to my associates that we employ Herbert's efficient and dedicated services on a permanent basis, which will allow us to work closely together.'

There were smiles of joy all around. The conversation lasted for another hour or so until I called a halt to it, and we parted warmly. I had passed another test of trustworthiness, and this time set by the entire family.

Cukurs accompanied me to the gate of his fortress.

'Tomorrow I'm flying to Montevideo,' I told him. 'I'll be staying at the Victoria Plaza Hotel, a first-class place. Send me a telegram when you're arriving. I hope to see you soon in Uruguay, so that we can wind up our business there.'

11
HE TAKES THE BAIT

THE MOVE from colourful, lively São Paulo to the tranquil, almost European Montevideo evoked in me great longings for my family.

A month had passed since I had last seen my wife, little daughter and son. A whole month without any contact – no phone call, no letter, just a brief line in the coded letters sent from Europe, with the cryptic, general sentence, 'All is well. Sending you our warm and loving regards.' And I knew that every time a letter of mine landed in the PO box in Paris or Rotterdam, one of my colleagues would telephone my wife and give her my regards. And that was that. My son was four at the time, and missed his father terribly. In cahoots with my wife, one of my friends telephoned, pretending to be me. The conversation lasted only a few seconds. My son, full of joy, had started pouring out his tales, but after a few sentences realized that he was being lied to. 'I want Daddy,' he started screaming and throwing a temper tantrum. 'My Daddy!' Our wives are the true heroes of all these affairs, but they will always remain anonymous.

Montevideo welcomed me with mild warm, spring weather. I used the following days to become acquainted with this city perched on the bank of the Rio de la Plata. The 135 kilometres of a most beautiful beach, stretching from Punta Brava to Punta del Este, made this town and its surroundings a popular and famous holiday resort – the South American Riviera.

Punta del Este had gained world renown following the famous clash in 1939 between the German battleship *Graf Spee* and the British Royal Navy. During the first months of the Second World War, the speedy battleship had operated in the

Atlantic Ocean, until the British navy located its precise position, and the hunt had started. The commander of the ship realized that he stood no chance of surviving a confrontation with the British fleet, and fled into the estuary of the Rio de la Plata. He soon found out that this move, in fact, meant the end of the war for him, since he had no chance of breaking through the circle of steel the British navy had set up just outside Uruguay's territorial waters. He therefore gave the order for his men to scuttle the large battleship in the river, opposite Punta del Este, and abandon it.

I took up residence in the Victoria Plaza Hotel, in the large Plaza Independencia in the centre of town. From my lofty window I had a panoramic view of the town. On the western part of the harbour stood a hillock, approximately 130 metres high, on which the Spaniards had built a fortress to defend the place against Portuguese raiders. The town took its name from this hillock: I see a mountain – Montevideo.

Below me, in Independence Square, the bronze figure of the father of the Uruguayan nation, General Artigas, perched atop a bronze stallion, watched over the traffic and tumult of this town that had more of a European character than a South American one. At the car rental agency Sudamcar, on the other side of the square, I managed to get hold of a relatively new Chevrolet. It was painted a shocking pink, which did not fit well with the respectable image I was trying to convey. I rented it anyway, since it was the only large car available and was by far more representative than the common VW Beetle.

I gave several real-estate agents headaches with my search for a house, of which I saw quite a few before deciding to focus my efforts in the Carrasco holiday resort neighbourhood. It had a large concentration of fairly isolated and empty holiday homes, a few restaurants and a casino. The airport also lay nearby, which was a major advantage in case something went wrong during our operation.

I hoped that the real-estate agents I had dealings with would take me seriously despite the shocking-pink Chevrolet I arrived in for our meetings. Now I must really look like an old playboy, I thought and smiled to myself, as

I was being driven through town in one of the realtors' Jaguar convertible. I told all of them a similar story, and said I would make another appointment with them in a few days. 'I'm waiting for my partner,' I explained. 'The minute he arrives I'll get in touch with you.'

The plan was slowly gaining momentum, and one day I found a telegram from Cukurs waiting for me at the hotel. 'Arriving Friday, October 16. Varig flight from São Paulo.'

I picked him up at the airport, and we greeted each other like old friends.

'I'm glad you came. I need your expertise,' I told him.

Cukurs brimmed with joy. This was the first time he had left Brazil since arriving there as a refugee in 1946. But he still maintained his high alert. 'The gun is with me,' he informed, and patted a bulky protrusion under his jacket. This was long before sky piracy turned the boarding of a plane into a lengthy ritual of rigorous security checks. In the 1960s no one had thought of the possibility of putting a gun to the pilot's head and declaring in a tense voice, 'This is a hijacking!'

'It was a pleasant flight, and I had no problems with the passport controls,' he announced. In order to appear a man of the world, Cukurs had purchased a cheap new suit, as well as a few relatively appropriate shirts. We exchanged a few more pleasantries, and I asked after his charming wife, children, daughter-in-law, and his business in Interlagos. We then climbed into the car, and drove into town.

Cukurs savoured every minute – he was undoubtedly in seventh heaven. It was evident in the way he settled in the soft seat of the Chevrolet, placed his elbow on the window, leaned back comfortably, and devoured everything the car passed.

'Check in, go up to your room, refresh yourself, and then to work,' I suggested once I parked outside the hotel.

A short while later we were in the large car again, on our way to survey the housing market. Once more we negotiated with an assortment of realtors the lease terms of various houses. We were looking for an isolated house, in good condition, that could serve me and my mysterious associates as a central office for our businesses in South America.

Cukurs never questioned the decision to look for a house rather than an office in a normal office building. He cooperated like a good trooper, loyal and obedient, who followed orders and did not ask too many questions. I left all the negotiations with the agents to Cukurs because I wanted to convince him that I really needed him, and also because I was personally sick and tired of these negotiations.

In the end we did not find a suitable house. The choice of rental houses Montevideo had to offer in the autumn of 1964 was fairly poor. What we liked was exorbitantly expensive, and the rest did not suit our needs.

'It's not bad,' I explained to Cukurs. 'That is how it is in business. Sometimes everything falls into place at once. Sometimes you have to wait. We wait. We have patience.'

We also had plenty of free time on our hands. We ate a leisurely rich lunch at a nice restaurant, during which Cukurs showed me his passport with great pride. I seized the opportunity and leafing through, closely studied all the details in it.

We also used the evenings to have fun, for instance paying a visit to the local casino. Cukurs was beside himself. Truth be known, though, compared with similar establishments in Europe, such as Monte Carlo or Baden Baden, this gambling house was rather dismal. But for him it was an excursion to the world of luxury and amusement, and he enjoyed every minute of it. I myself am no great gambler, and previous such visits had always ended with me leaving a small sum of money to the house. But this time Lady Luck was on my side. After a few minutes at the roulette table, I won a fairly substantial amount – about US$200.

'This is your share.' I handed Cukurs half of the win.

'How come? Herr Anton, you gambled with your money, and you won. This isn't mine.'

'Herbert, we are partners after all,' I said, trying to end the discussion.

But Cukurs still brought up a few counterarguments before he finally capitulated and took the money. 'You see, Herr Anton, money goes to money,' he said, and the way he pronounced my name smacked of dependency.

The following day we drove along the coast to Punta del Este. On the way there we drove through many small holiday villages, among them Atlantida and Piriapolis, South American household names for seaside holidays. We stopped for a fine lunch at an outdoor restaurant, during which Cukurs tried to appear calm, but I felt he was tense. Very tense. Only months later did I find out that it was during this lunch that Cukurs came to the conclusion that he was being followed. His wife mentioned it after Cukurs' death, in a conversation with a Brazilian journalist.

'When my husband returned from his first business trip to Uruguay with that Austrian Kuenzle,' Milda Cukurs recalled, 'Herbert told me that he had noticed his followers. It happened during the lunch he and Kuenzle had at a large restaurant called Suizo Bungalow in Punta del Este. Herbert had noticed a group of four young people who looked Jewish – two women and two men. They were sitting a few tables away from Herbert and Kuenzle, spoke in loud voices, and made much noise, as is typical of Jews.'

My memories of this event, which disturbed Cukurs so much that he had to share his concerns with his wife, are somewhat different. With all due respect to Cukurs' caution and to his senses that had been sharpened by 20 years of flight, I cannot remember anything extraordinary happening during that lunch. And yet, this little episode shows how alert Cukurs remained, even in my company. In my view, by that stage Cukurs was suffering from advanced paranoia, which only heightened his alertness.

One night, as we ate dinner in a restaurant in Montevideo, Cukurs suddenly addressed our waiter, most probably putting me to the test again, saying, 'Redst du a bissl Yiddish?' (Do you speak a little Yiddish?).

Survivors of the Riga massacre had testified that Cukurs not only understood Yiddish, the language of his victims, but also spoke it. The waiter, who had clearly never heard a word of Yiddish in his life and was evidently not a Jew, did not understand what the diner wanted with him. Only when Cukurs spoke to him in Spanish again, with its foreign accent, did he realize that he was dealing here with tourists, who tend to behave strangely on their holidays.

At that dinner Cukurs and I summed up our joint endeavours in Uruguay.

'All in all I'm quite pleased, even though we haven't yet found what we are looking for,' I told him. 'Tomorrow I'm flying back to Europe. As you know, I have other businesses in different parts of the world which demand my presence and active involvement. But this trip to South America, and very much thanks to your support and assistance, has convinced me that tourism is about to blossom here, and I want to be in on it. I'm going to recommend to my associates that they invest large sums of money here, stressing the advantages of already having here a dedicated and alert colleague like yourself.'

I noted with satisfaction how much he liked my compliments.

'I reckon I'll be back here at the beginning of next year with the investment capital. Are you interested in becoming part of these enterprises?'

His reply was swift and positive.

'Fine, Herbert,' I carried on with my summation. 'We shall of course cover all your expenses, and reward you handsomely for your efforts. By the way, you know how accountants are – mine always gives me hell for forgetting my receipts. So once you return home, please send the receipts to my office in Rotterdam, especially the São Paulo–Montevideo return flight ticket. After all, it's a considerable amount of money, and we can't claim it as expenses without the actual ticket.'

Cukurs promised to do so, and to keep in touch until I returned and called him up.

The next morning we parted like two good, old friends.

'A pleasant flight, Herr Anton, and see you soon,' he said before boarding the plane back to São Paulo.

'Best regards to your wife. We'll definitely meet again before long,' I said, and went to the departure lounge, where I waited for the plane that would take me on the long and exhausting flight back to Europe.

12
PREPARING FOR THE EXECUTION

PARIS WELCOMED me with all the varied hues of autumn, which only magnified the beauty of the city, and with myriad falling leaves. The chilly evening wind was already announcing the onslaught of winter.

'Now I'm staying put for a few months, together with you,' I promised my wife. My little daughter and son were overjoyed to see me again, and soon forgot my long absence. But I did not come to Paris for a holiday. Planning the completion of the Cukurs operation still lay ahead of us.

In the apartment made available to us on the Avenue de Versailles, a hefty file awaited me. My friend Adi had gathered in it all the letters I had sent from Brazil and Uruguay to the two addresses in Paris and Rotterdam. The overt and covert information they contained served as the basis of a report that detailed everything I had done in South America, and all the information I had gathered in preparation for the final act.

The bulky file was well-arranged and comprehensive. It contained a brief description of Cukurs' crimes, and his flight to Brazil; an explanation of Cukurs' habits; a depiction of his family, home and its surroundings; the development of the relationships between me, Anton Kuenzle, and Cukurs; detailed descriptions of our joint trips; as well as numerous operational details that to the outsider may seem superfluous, yet every time prove their significance anew: problems that may arise when renting a vehicle in Brazil; operational difficulties that could be caused by the scarcity of suitable rental cars in Uruguay; the house-rental procedure in Montevideo; the documents required when checking into a hotel.

I also included maps of the relevant cities, lists of hotels, procedures for entering and departing from the countries in the region, escape routes, and much more; a large volume, summing up in words and photographs my 40 days of operating on the other side of the ocean. It concluded with my outline of operational options and my recommendations for our next moves. I emphasized repeatedly that we were dealing here with a highly mistrustful man, acutely vigilant, armed with a gun, and of great physical strength.

I pointed out that a distant sniper shot was not, in my opinion at least, a suitable option, both because of the noise and because it would not allow us to give him the *coup de grâce.*

I also rejected the use of poison in order to end the life of the Monster of Riga. I gave a detailed account of the so-called drinking night I had set up at the Japanese nightclub in São Paulo, a night in which Cukurs had stayed sober to the very end. I mentioned his strange habit of sipping his drink in an ever-so-slow, almost nerve-wracking fashion, most probably his way of protecting himself against tranquilizers or poison.

'Therefore,' I concluded, 'I believe that the best way is to lure him into a house where an elimination unit would be waiting for him. From my intense and intimate acquaintance with The Deceased, and from the numerous hours we have spent together, which have included many visits to various rental sites, I am convinced that he will enter any house I do. He trusts me.'

The full report was submitted to Yoav, the commander, as well as to Michael and Aryeh, who had accompanied the operation from the outset.

'Congratulations on a great job,' Yoav complimented me at another meeting in the apartment. 'With your information, we must now consider how to utilize all this data and bring this operation to a successful conclusion.'

But it did not take us long to agree on a plan, since Yoav basically accepted my recommendations.

'Yitzhak was there, he knows the man, and if he thinks that this is the best way, I'm all for it,' he said. 'We'll lead him into a trap, overpower him, read him the verdict in the name of his 30,000 victims, and carry out the execution there and then.'

I was pleased. Yes, I felt great satisfaction at Yoav's short summation that was also an expression of deep appreciation of the work I had done over the last weeks.

'Now we must move from planning to preparations. We must put together the right team, establish a timetable, and everything of course subject to the latest developments on the ground,' he said, and set up the time for our next meet.

But the meeting took place earlier than planned, moved forward by the envelope covered in Brazilian stamps that arrived at the Rotterdam PO box on 9 November. The letter said,

> Dear Herr Kuenzle,
> Following your request, I hereby enclose my flight ticket from São Paulo to Montevideo and back, as well as a few other receipts for various expenses. I hope you arrived well in Rotterdam, and that all is well with you. Hoping to see you soon.
> With friendship, yours, Herbert Cukurs.

If Cukurs had followed my instructions to forward me the flight ticket, it was fairly safe to assume that The Deceased had swallowed the hook along with the bait, I thought on my way to the Avenue de Versailles for another meeting at the apartment. So all the work in South America had not come to naught. Cukurs had developed a dependency on me, Anton. Now we could count on Cukurs' almost Prussian sense of discipline. Now he would do anything I asked him to.

Yoav had similar thoughts, and preparations for the last stage moved into a higher gear. On 31 December 1964, I sent Cukurs a short letter,

> Dear Herbert,
> I thank you for your letter, and for the receipts you sent. Thanks also in the name of my accountant. Everything here is running as it should, and as far as business is concerned, I have nothing to complain about. My associates are very pleased with the outcome of my trip to South America, to Brazil and Uruguay. I intend to return to South America in the coming weeks, in order

to implement and realize various investment plans, including the ones you have taken some part in.

I intend to take care of some matters in Uruguay and Chile during this trip. I shall therefore be grateful to you if you could manage soon after receiving this letter to make the necessary arrangements for a business trip to these two countries, and obtain the appropriate entry visas. I'm enclosing a bankers cheque for US$100 to cover your expenses. Additional details, including the precise date, will be sent later. Please inform me by telegram when all the necessary papers are in your hands, and you are ready for the trip.

A happy new year to you and your family. Hope to see you soon,

Your friend, Anton Kuenzle

In the meantime, a professional team was put together. Five Mossad men had been assigned to the small unit that was to act in Uruguay. Yoav, our experienced and capable commander was put in charge of the operation.

My friend, Oswald Taussig, was also equipped with an Austrian passport. Taussig had amassed considerable experience in clandestine operations during the time he had served with the Etzel, the more radical Jewish underground during the years of strife and struggle that eventually led to the establishment of the State of Israel. Only after the whole operation was over did I find out that he had a personal connection to this operation. His mother and grandmother had been born in Riga, and he had had quite a large family in the Latvian capital. They were all killed by Cukurs and his men.

Arieh, Yoav's right-hand man, also had substantial experience. The youngest of the participants was Dova'le. He was born in one of the older settlements in the Jezreel Valley, and had served in the acclaimed 101 parachutists unit, which provided him with plenty of experience in field operations. It was he who one year earlier had checked out and verified the fact that Cukurs lived under his own name in São Paulo, and for him too this mission was somehow the closing of a circle. Michael and Adi were assigned to take care of all the logistics in Europe involved in the execution of a Nazi war criminal in South America.

There was no shortage of problems, but the team was experienced and within a few days a working paper had been prepared, divided into sections and subsections, which constituted the operation order. It was based on the data I had gathered and on the detailed report I had written after my return, and specified each of our roles. The maps I had brought allowed us to examine different traffic routes through Montevideo, and we decided to concentrate our search for a suitable house in the area I had recommended.

Every member of the team adopted an identity with which he could enter and exit Uruguay, and spent long hours on developing his new personal cover story. The preparations also included learning a few basic sentences in Spanish and Portuguese. It was winter in Europe, but we prepared ourselves for a stay in the hot South American summer. Adi ran around and kept very busy, and saw to it that the team went on its way well-equipped with the various necessary currencies.

There were still numerous problems we had to take care of, and dozens of difficulties to overcome, all aimed at ascertaining that the mission would be completed without any hitches or complications.

Yoav, Arieh, Oswald and Dova'le underwent special karate training in order to be able to jump Cukurs and immediately overpower him as he entered the house I would lead him into. The training was given by Immi, one of Israel's best hand-to-hand combat trainers, a strong, hefty man with the graceful movements of a dancer. Immi never asked why, nor did he dwell too much on the request he had received, namely to take a group of men and teach them how to fell a man with one well-aimed blow. He did see to it, however, that the four not-so-young men he had been assigned practised the motions over and again until they reached a satisfactory level of performance. It was a pity, though, that he never found out whose neck his pupils would be breaking, for this taciturn karate instructor also had a long account with the Nazis.

Immi had been among the 400 illegal passengers on board the small ship *Stefano* that had managed to flee the European inferno at the last minute. The ship left the port of Bratislava on the Danube River under a Bulgarian flag, with a Russian captain, and Greek sailors. The passengers, who held forged Paraguayan passports, were mostly members of the Zionist Betar youth movement, and from central Europe. There were also several dozen German and Czech Jews from Dachau and other concentration camps who, by a rare chain of coincidences, had succeeded in escaping the camps and the bitter fate that befell the Jews of Europe.

The ship had been renamed *Pancho*, after the nickname of Reuven Franco, who was active in the illegal immigration of Jews to British Mandate Palestine. After four months of wandering down the Danube, in September 1940, the ship finally sailed into the Black Sea. However, the plight of its passengers was far from over. Turkey drove the ship and its passengers away as if were infested with the plague. Greece, concerned with the drums of war that came from fascist Italy, also proved no help at all. Money was running out. The food and water supplies dwindled by the day. But the strong will to reach the Land of Israel drove the *Pancho* onward, to the east.

Somewhere near the island of Rhodes the beat-up ship was stopped by an Italian navy torpedo boat.

'Are you out of your minds?' boomed the voice of the Italian captain on the bullhorn. 'You're in the middle of a minefield!'

The frightened passengers realized that it was only the ship's small size and relatively high hull that had saved it from a deadly collision with the sea mines. Ignoring everything the fascist flag that flew proudly from his ship's mast stood for, the Italian captain helped the *Pancho* navigate safely out of the minefield. Having made sure that they were out of danger, he said a friendly goodbye to the illegal immigrants and wholeheartedly wished them success.

But misfortune did not leave them, for a few hours later a boiler exploded in the engine room. The passengers improvised sails from blankets and sheets, and the *Pancho* continued its slow journey eastward, to the Land of Israel.

The *Pancho*'s troubled voyage ended long before the shores of the promised land were even visible. On 9 October 1940, during a storm, the ship became stranded on a sandbar, and its hundreds of passengers had to abandon it. The nearby 4-square-kilometre deserted Greek island, Kamilonisi, somewhere between Rhodes and Crete, provided them with temporary refuge. The avidly Zionist passengers hoisted the Star of David flag atop the highest hillock, wrote SOS on the rocks, and lit fires, in the hope that a passing plane would spot their distress signals. The stranded ate what little they had salvaged from the ship's wreckage, and drank rainwater that had gathered in the nooks and crannies of the rocks.

'If we wait until someone finds us, they'll find only skeletons,' Immi told his friends. 'We must try and get help.'

Together with four other strong young men, Immi dislodged a small rowboat from the remnants of the ship. They took a little food and water, and rowed into the open sea. They parted from their friends, not knowing that another three years would pass before they met again.

The shipwrecked passengers spent another ten days among the rocks of Kamilonisi before an Italian navy destroyer rescued them and brought them to a provisional camp in southern Italy. They stayed there for three years, under harsh conditions. Only the allied forces' invasion of Italy in 1943 ended their odyssey. In a gesture of goodwill, the British allowed the *Pancho* passengers, who had fled Europe in the summer of 1940, to reach their original destination, the Land of Israel.

As for the five rowing young men, they spent days in the open sea, until finally they were picked up by a British destroyer. They told the British captain about their voyage, and he passed on the information. Immi and his friends joined the destroyer's crew, and sailed with it to its base in Alexandria. Immi immediately went to the recruitment office of the Czech Free Army, and volunteered to fight against the Nazis. After the war ended, he went to Palestine, and with the establishment of the state, joined the IDF as a close-combat instructor. Almost 25 years after he had fled the Nazis, he was training a team of men who were about to settle the account with one of the worst sadists who had served in the Nazi death machine. And Immi pushed them hard, until they had mastered the art of felling a man in one blow.

'Remember, The Deceased is a strong man, and he's always armed,' I kept reminding my friends – like the old Cato who completed every speech he made at the Roman senate with the immortal sentence 'And by the way, I think Carthage must be destroyed.'

'Yitzhak exaggerates a bit. We'll overcome Cukurs without problems,' they responded, as they practised for the thousandth time the deadly motion.

On 20 January 1956, a letter landed in my PO box in Rotterdam. By its stamp it had been sent from São Paulo nine days earlier.

> Herr Kuenzle,
> I completed all the arrangements as you asked. I have the passport, including the visas for Uruguay and Chile. Waiting for your arrival, and for further details concerning our joint business trip.
>
> With friendship, Herbert Cukurs

'All right. We're entering the final stage,' said Yoav after hearing my report about the latest developments. He called another meeting at the Avenue de Versailles apartment. The entire team was there, and I recall a rather matter-of-fact atmosphere, almost devoid of emotion. We were all aware that we were going to take the life of a man, but none of us had any doubt that this was the just punishment for the sadistic criminal, Herbert Cukurs.

During those same days the Israeli spymaster Eli Cohen was arrested in Damascus, a fact that inevitably influenced our mood. According to the Syrian press, which published segments of his interrogation, Eli Cohen had admitted that one of his missions in Damascus was to locate Nazi war criminals who were hiding there. The best known of them was Alois Brunner, who continued to lead a peaceful life in the Syrian capital up to the mid-1990s, after which he disappeared without a trace.

We went over the plan once more. The timetable was flexible, and could be adjusted to fit changing circumstances.

'The day after tomorrow Yitzhak will wire Cukurs about his return to South America,' said Yoav. 'Where and when would you like to meet him?' he asked me.

'In the transit lounge of São Paulo airport,' I decided, and explained, 'Like that I save myself the trouble of trying to obtain another visa to Brazil. And since I have some knowledge of South American mentality and efficiency, I intend to send the telegram today already, and let him know in plenty of time of our meeting in four days, on 28 January.'

'Best of luck,' said Yoav and raised his glass. He had never been a man of many words. 'Best of luck, *l'chaim*,' echoed the rest of us.

Three days later Anton Kuenzle sat in an Air France airplane, and once more crossed the Atlantic Ocean.

'It's going to be a short trip this time,' I promised my wife the evening before. 'This time it's going to take much less than 40 days.'

13
CAUGHT ON CAMERA

THE WARM winter clothes of the Boeing passengers from cold Paris became a burden the moment the doors of the plane opened in São Paulo. The gush of hot air that burst in made it evident that despite the date, 28 January 1965, we had landed right in the tropical summer of the southern hemisphere.

'Please allow the passengers whose destination is São Paulo to disembark first,' requested the flight attendant on the PA system. 'Passengers flying on with us to Buenos Aires are requested to go to the transit lounge until the aircraft has been refuelled.'

Obedient as ever, I waited until all the São Paulo passengers left, and then got up from my seat.

'Hello, Herr Anton. I am here!' I heard Cukurs' familiar voice. It sounded somewhat joyful, maybe because it was a quarter of an octave higher than usual. I looked down to the bottom of the stairs. And what did I see? Herbert Cukurs, festively clad, wearing a colourful tie, holding something black in one hand, and waving happily with the other. How on earth did he manage to get in here, I wondered. This was a restricted area, and we were supposed to meet in the transit lounge. The pilots' fraternity must have gotten him a security pass for this area. He must know a pilot who knows a pilot whose cousin was the airport's director...

But my thoughts were cut off abruptly when I realized that the black object in his hand was a small movie camera. A camera? What was going on here? This meant that Cukurs was actually filming me, immortalizing my image on 8mm celluloid! Instinctively I raised my hand as if in greeting, but the motion was actually intended to hide from the camera lens some of my more distinguishing features, my baldness, for instance.

He'll never be rid of his suspicions, which was why he was filming me, I thought with concern. Outwardly, though, I maintained the expression of a passenger who was about to meet his good, old friend whom he had not seen for months, and who had come a long way to welcome him.

I was fully convinced that this was yet another one of Cukurs' security exercises, intended to test my honourable intentions. One false move that might be interpreted as an attempt to hide from the camera and all my months-long efforts to win his trust would come to naught.

I found out only after the operation was over how right I was in my diagnosis. Despite all the evidence to the contrary, Cukurs had never really stopped mistrusting me. He had brought the movie camera along as an insurance policy.

'My husband, Herbert, told me that he had filmed Anton Kuenzle coming off the plane,' Milda Cukurs said a few weeks later. 'My husband emphasized that if anything bad were to happen to him in the near future, then it was this man, Kuenzle, seen here waving so jovially, who would bear direct and sole responsibility for it.'

I descended the stairs quickly and kept waving my hand. The faster I neared Cukurs, the shorter the time my rounded frame would remain in focus and therefore discernible, and once I reached him, he would have to stop filming.

'I'm so glad to see you, Herbert,' I said warmly, and shook his hand firmly.

'Me too,' responded Cukurs, who of course had to stop filming or appear impolite. 'We are so lucky. We almost missed one another. I received your telegram only this morning.'

How fortunate that I had not sent the telegram only two days before my flight, as Yoav had suggested, I thought. Cukurs would only have received it in two days' time, and I would have had to run around Buenos Aires like a rabbit in order to obtain a visa to Brazil, and the whole timetable would have been off. Not to mention the other complications that could have arisen.

'Let's go and have something to drink. There's something important I must tell you,' I said to Cukurs, and led the way to the transit lounge. 'My associates and I have decided to invest heavily in South America. I'm sure you'll be interested in hearing the details of how you can take part in our plans.'

'I have a little problem,' Cukurs opened once we sat over our steaming *cafezinho* in the transit lounge's cafeteria. 'My papers aren't ready yet,' he said, his eyes downcast. 'I still have a few formalities I must complete before I can join you on your trip to one of the neighbouring countries.'

I was livid, and I made no secret of it. I was concerned about our timetable, since at this stage, with the entire team already mobilized, any delay could actually jeopardize the whole operation.

'How could you do this?' I scolded Cukurs like a stern teacher would an errant pupil. 'And you say you want to be a businessman? I'm a businessman, and I stick by my word! This is how business is run. Didn't you write me that you'd completed all the formalities and gotten all the necessary papers? You wrote me that all your papers were in order. That means that everything is ready, and we can move forward!'

With every angry sentence I spat out, he lowered his eyes further, until he looked like a miserable and guilty poodle who has peed on the carpet.

'I want you to know that I'm very, very disappointed,' I said, ending my short sermon.

It would be an exaggeration to say that the tough Cukurs was on the verge of tears, but he was definitely embarrassed. First, because it must have been years since anybody had scolded him like this, and second, because he was fearful of losing the opportunity to join the business world and miss his chance of economic salvation. Of course, he had no way of knowing that the last thing on my mind was to sever our relations because of his little lie about the papers. True, this was an unexpected drawback, but it also had some advantage as far as I was concerned, since it actually strengthened my position. Once I was convinced that my pedagogic goal had been achieved, I changed to a milder tone of voice. For his part, Cukurs promised on all that was dear to him that this had been a one-off slip-up. I accepted his explanation with magnanimity.

'We've done some market research in recent months,' I informed Cukurs. 'My associates and I have come to the conclusion that Brazil isn't politically stable enough at the moment, and that Uruguay and Chile are preferable for our purposes. That is why I shall concentrate on these two countries during this visit. I would like you to accompany me on the trips to Montevideo and Santiago de Chile.'

Cukurs listened intently, clearly taking pleasure in my reasoning for needing him. After all, who does not love to hear how indispensable they are? And this was precisely what I told him repeatedly in the transit lounge of São Paulo airport. Then I handed him a relatively large amount of money, sufficient 'to complete your preparations, and purchase the flight tickets to Montevideo and Santiago'.

'Do you by any chance have the names of the hotels where we'll be staying in Montevideo and Santiago?' Cukurs inquired, as if he were a travel agent.

Cautious! The bastard is forever cautious. He was still trying to find out whether this really was a well-planned and properly prepared business trip.

'Do you have a pen?' I asked. 'Then write it down!' And I proceeded to dictate the list to him, including the addresses and telephone numbers, for I had all these details well-prepared in my mind beforehand.

'Passengers on Air France flight from Paris to Buenos Aires are requested to go to terminal A in order to return to the aircraft...' came the announcement over the transit lounge speakers.

'That's it, Herbert. I must go. Let me know when you're arriving, and don't let me down.' The parting sentence, accompanied by a slap on his shoulder, made it clear to him that I indeed forgave him, but also that it should never, ever happen again. I had no doubt that he would hurry and complete all the necessary arrangements, and inform me immediately when he was ready.

I was stuck in Buenos Aires for a whole week. An

unexpected post and telephone strike broke out the day after my arrival in the Argentinean capital. How was I expected to work under such conditions and run operations that needed so much coordination, I wondered.

I used the idle time for touring. I took a flight to Mar del Plata, a popular holiday resort. On the way out, the plane flew right into the worst thunder and lightning storm I had ever experienced. The pilot must have decided that there was a limit to the risks he was willing to take, or maybe he had some unfinished personal business at home; whatever, he turned the plane around and flew back to Buenos Aires. The airline sent us to our destination by train.

The short break I took in Mar del Plata turned out to be a disappointment. The shabby place reminded me of run-down holiday resorts in France or Belgium that remained stuck in the 1930s. It was no wonder that my longings for home reached new heights.

I returned to Buenos Aires by plane, this time landing on time and in the right airport. I spent the next days anxiously waiting for Cukurs' telegram to arrive so that we could get on with our plans. Over five months had passed since that meeting in the Paris apartment where I had heard Cukurs' name for the very first time. During these five months, this despicable man had taken a central place in my life. But now I had had enough! He should sort out his arrangements and get here now. I completely overlooked the absurdity of the situation, in which in my mind I urged him to come quickly only to meet his demise.

To pass the time, I took to walking the streets of Buenos Aires, and to spending long hours in the lovely Café Aguila, which I knew from previous visits. I also saw folklore performances at a small club not far from the Plaza San Martin. But above all I waited for the post and telephone strike to be over. I hoped they would reach a settlement soon. Management should give in a little, and the trade unions should demonstrate some flexibility, and let them sign a new agreement and start operating the telephone exchanges and telegram offices again.

Whether it was because of my prayer or because the two

sides had finally reached an accord, the strike was over, and at midday, 5 February, when I returned to my hotel from yet another round of wandering through the city, a telegram was waiting for me at the reception desk.

> Glad to inform you that all the preparations are complete. I have the documents and the visa. Waiting to hear from you as to where and when I join you.
>
> With friendship, yours, Herbert

A few minutes later a business telegram made its way from Buenos Aires to Paris.

> Negotiations have finished, and the transaction is about to take place. Request you send urgently the team of experts in order to complete this transaction successfully.
>
> Anton

14
WAITING FOR CUKURS

THE INFLUX of tourists to Argentina that week included several European citizens for whom any connection between the information in their passports and reality was purely accidental. First to arrive was Oswald, a man in his forties, who presented an Austrian passport to the border control officer. Shortly after, Arieh, Yoav and Dova'le landed in the Argentinean capital. The members of the team took up residence in different quarters of the city.

Our coordination meetings took place at side tables of Buenos Aires' crowded cafés. We spoke quietly, so that we could converse freely in Hebrew, as was our wont. I informed the others of all the latest developments, and despite their intensive karate training, I kept reminding them not to underestimate Cukurs.

'He's like a wild animal. The minute he senses that he is trapped, he'll muster all his strength. And believe you me – despite almost reaching the age of 65, he's still quite strong.'

On 10 February 1965, I moved to Montevideo. Oswald followed me shortly, took residence in the luxurious Nogaro Hotel, and rented a green VW Beetle.

Oswald and I soon realized that we were facing two major problems. The first was the rental of reliable cars that would not stall on us at the most critical moments of the operation. It seemed to be an impossible task. The word 'maintenance' did not seem to exist in the vocabulary of the car-rental agencies. It was February, the end of Uruguay's summer, and the rental cars that had been used to the last day of the vacation were in desperate need of some serious maintenance and repair work, like changing tyres and cleaning the carburettors.

But the car rental was nothing compared to our other problem – the inexplicable scarcity of rental homes suitable for our purposes. Every morning I scanned the real-estate columns in the local newspapers. Oswald and I scoured the town from one end to the other. We employed the best real-estate agents. And despite all our efforts, we were still unable to locate a house that fulfilled our requirements. It had to be presentable, in order to make the right impression on Cukurs, conveniently located with easy access and escape routes, and surrounded by a garden large enough to allow us to do our job without the unwanted interference of the neighbours, let alone of law-enforcement agents.

In the meantime we managed to find another VW Beetle in relatively good condition, and the other members of the team who had arrived in Montevideo on separate flights, and taken up residence, had started to get acquainted with the city. Spy movies depict such activities in glowing colours, but in real life they are quite grey, exhausting and more often than not also boring. The team members found their way around, and memorized major thoroughfares and how to get from one end of the town to the other. They studied the peculiar customs of Uruguayan drivers, marked traffic lights, and located potential meeting points. But above all, the members of the team passed many hours in a nerve-wracking wait.

Throughout those endless days we all observed one primal rule – not to become involved with the law, not even by committing a parking violation, and not to draw any attention to ourselves. The last thing we needed was to be registered in some police file, or to have a legal entanglement. That would be utterly superfluous and harmful in every way.

The days passed, and I became concerned. Despite our ceaseless searches and efforts, we still had not found our house. Then Oswald came one morning and announced, 'I think I found something more or less suitable. I met this Greek guy, Dionysos Mavèrides, and told him the usual story about the house I want to rent so that I can spend a couple of pleasant months there with my wife. So he shows me this house, which is unfortunately way too big. It is two storeys high, and not really suitable. Apparently I must have left such a good impression on him that he introduces me to his friend Antonio Jimenez, and this Jimenez may have something that will solve our problems.'

We all went to see the place, taking care of course not to draw too much attention to ourselves. It was a small house, named Casa Cubertini, on Cartagena Street (which instantly brought Old Cato and his nagging sentence back to mind), in the Carrasco Quarter, only two streets away from the office of the real-estate agent with the white Jaguar.

Classic it was not, I thought when I first saw the place. The neighbouring streets were fairly quiet, and traffic was scarce, which was the only advantage I could see. A dirt road led to the house, which appeared neglected and not quite finished. There were no blinds on the windows, and the rooms were unfurnished. The living room walls were covered in a tasteless mosaic of pink and black tiles, and the small fireplace looked like it had never experienced burning logs. The sea was nearby, some 100 metres or so, and the sound of the waves could be heard. All things considered, we would have taken the house without any further hesitation, but the place had one major additional drawback. A short distance from it, not more than 30 metres away, a group of builders were busy renovating another house. The previous tenants of the Casa Cubertini had evidently been no garden lovers, since the place was utterly bereft of shrubs or trees, which gave the builders a clear view of the entrance to the house.

'So what do you think?' asked Yoav, not concealing his doubts. I weighed the odds. Should we continue our search for exactly the right house, or should we take into account the pressure of our timetable and, in the absence of a better solution, compromise and make do with what we had?

'I think it can work,' I said finally after some more deliberation. 'Needless to say, it would be preferable to find something more suitable, but we can manage with this one. We'll come here on the house tour I'll set up. Of course, if I'm all polite and start with the "after you" business, I doubt he'll enter the house. He's incredibly cautious. He'll never agree to be the first to enter a house he's never set foot in. But there's a solution. I'll tell him that this is our temporary office here, get out of the car and, without waiting for him, walk right up to the entrance, open the door and go inside. Cukurs is bound to follow me. I'm sure he'll come into the house without a problem. What happens once he's inside and the door is closed behind him is entirely up to you.'

Yoav listened to my words. He had known me for years and relied on my judgement. If I said that it was doable, despite the fact that the location was far from being ideal, then it was doable.

'I agree. Okay, Oswald, we've reached a decision. Go to your Greek or whoever it is, pay the rent, and sign the contract.'

With Yoav's approval, Taussig left in a hurry. He rented the house for two months, paid most of the rent in cash, in local currency, and promised to pay the rest in the next few days.

Now that we had the house, we were able to set a precise timetable.

'23 February is D-Day,' Yoav announced. 'Let it be with luck!'

On the same evening I sent a telegram to São Paulo.

> Dear Herbert,
> Business running well. Your help needed. I'll be glad if you could join me in Montevideo on the morning of 23 February.
>
> As always, yours, Anton

Sometimes telegraph services in South America can actually be efficient. The next day I found Cukurs' response in my pigeonhole at the reception desk at the Victoria Plaza Hotel.

> Dear Anton,
> Arriving by Varig flight on the 23rd.
>
> Yours, Herbert

Some hours later an update arrived.

Dear Anton,
Arriving on Air France flight 083, and not as stated in previous telegram.
With friendship, Yours, Herbert

I reserved a room for him at my hotel, and together with the rest of the team went over all the details again and again. Every day I scanned all the newspapers, updating myself on the latest events in Uruguay. I spoke no Spanish, but thanks to the many Latin classes I had had to endure in my youth as a pupil in the high school for the humanities in Germany, I was able to decipher the words. This was how I accidentally stumbled on a public announcement stating that a major artery of the city would be closed for repair works in the coming days. I informed the other members of the team, and we adjusted our plans accordingly.

Led by Yoav, the team went over the route and the timetable, rehearsing it over and again. Hard in training, easy in battle – the old cliché, so familiar to every Israeli from basic training, is valid not only when shots are being fired.

Every one of us prepared a small emergency suitcase for the hasty retreat. We did not want to be held back by anything, definitely not by having to check out of the hotel or pack our belongings.

Oswald surveyed many of Montevideo's luggage stores. He had very specific requirements, and the best salespeople in this branch tried to oblige him, to no avail. He was looking for a large travelling trunk, the kind that features in travel books from the nineteenth century, the kind Thomas Cook passengers had taken along, packing therein half of their household. He had almost given up when he finally found the right trunk in a store two streets away from the US embassy.

'The customer was quite demanding, almost a nuisance,' recalled the salesman in the luggage store sometime later, when questioned. 'He had a tape-measure with him, and measured every trunk – length, width and depth. He stood there for 20 minutes, taking measurements of every trunk and suitcase we had in stock, and asking every so often whether we had something larger. In the end he settled on one trunk, and at the same time, also purchased two carpets. He paid 720 pesos for the trunk, and another 900 pesos for the carpets. Since the trunk did not fit into his VW, I ordered a delivery truck for him, which transported the trunk to a house on Cartagena Street in the Carrasco Quarter.'

I myself was busy taking care of many minor details. I checked my bill so far at the hotel, and discovered that I had amassed a pretty hefty one. Since such a bill could arouse the suspicion of the cashier, I settled it immediately, and paid in advance for the following days both for my own room and the additional one I had reserved. I did the same thing at the car-rental agency, where I left a deposit large enough to cover the rental fees for a few more days. At the Lufthansa office I booked Cukurs and myself seats on the flight to Santiago for 25 February.

During the last days of preparation we stopped meeting as a group, and Yoav was my only contact.

'We are missing someone who really knows the area well, the mentality and the language,' said Yoav at one such meeting. 'To bring over one of our people would be too costly, and time is getting tight. So I turned to a friend of mine who works here, and he's going to help us. And during the operation we'll use him as a lookout from a distance, and so have another security and control position.'

On one of the last evenings, I made my way to the pleasant Malecon Restaurant, which I knew from previous visits. The place was chosen for the last coordination meeting of the entire team. Arieh arrived first. By pure coincidence the waiter led us to the very same table at which I had had dinner with Cukurs only a few months before.

'By the way,' I said to Arieh in passing, 'you're sitting on the very same seat The Deceased sat on.'

Arieh jumped up as if he had been bitten by a cobra. 'I don't believe in superstitions, but let's move to another table.'

But this was not the only peculiar thing that happened during that evening. Later on, as we were talking in low voices, trying not to attract attention, all of a sudden the waiter spoke to us.

'Shalom, friends,' he said in Hebrew, and although he

spoke only two words, his Hungarian accent was easily discernible. 'I served with the Fourth battalion of the Palmach, and was stationed in Nahariya,' he said, tightening the knot between the Jews of the Diaspora and the unofficial representatives of the State of Israel. We all laughed, but from that moment on we spoke in hushed voices, so that we could not be heard by anyone around.

On one of the last evenings before D-Day, Yoav and I had dinner together, and then went to the local Casino Park Rodo in order to alleviate some of the tension. Yoav, like I, was not a frequent visitor to such establishments. If anything, we were the antitheses of your typical gambler – we were circumspect, sensible and cautious. We never relied on luck, but rather on meticulous planning. But we just needed a complete change of atmosphere.

We bought some chips for a small amount of money, and went over to the roulette table. I'm still not sure why, but I placed my chips on number 23.

'*Nada mas, rien ne va plus*,' announced the croupier. The small ball rolled, skipped and hopped, and finally landed on . . . number 23!

'This means that someone up there likes the idea of our operation taking place on the 23rd,' I commented.

'Sure', responded Yoav, smiling. 'I don't believe in all these superstitions. But there's no doubt that this is an encouraging and positive omen.'

On the night of 22–23 February, I went to bed after having had a decent, yet not too heavy, dinner. I slept well that night, a deep sleep, loading the batteries for the next day, the crucial day, Judgement Day.

15
JUDGEMENT DAY

'THE BONN Government will Discuss Tomorrow the Investigation of Nazi Crimes,' announced the headline of one of Uruguay's newspapers on Tuesday, 23 February 1965. 'The West German government will discuss the report by Minister of Justice Dr Ewald Bucher, dealing with the possibility of examining all the material regarding Nazi crimes, and submitting it to the German courts before the period of limitation starts on 8 May.' Namely, in less than two months.

I must confess that I was glad to see this headline only many years later, when I gathered material on the Cukurs affair, and not as I waited on that morning of 23 February 1965 for Herbert Cukurs' arrival on Air France flight 083. The wheels of the large Boeing touched down on the asphalt-covered runway of Carrasco airport at precisely 9:30 a.m.

An exciting chapter in my life was about to come to an end. Six months of a constant war of wits, tension and uncertainty, and the tireless efforts invested in order to bring us to this moment.

I felt calm and composed, and not just because of my operational experience, but also due to the Librium I had taken. It's not that I needed a tranquilizer; the reason was much simpler. I had inherited from my father one particular trait that did not always go well with clandestine operations: I perspired heavily, especially on my head, and in my case, my bald spot. I was afraid that Cukurs would notice it, and suspect that I was nervous – maybe because of the unpleasant surprise I had prepared for him. In Argentina I went into a drugstore, where the chemist suggested I try out a brand new medication, Librium. I tested it first, making sure that it did indeed lessen my profuse sweating and had no unwarranted side-effects, such as behaviour or mind alteration. I had taken one pill that morning, before leaving for the airport.

From the visitors' gallery, hidden among other welcoming parties, I watched Cukurs emerge from the plane. He looked up to the gallery, searched for me, and when he detected my familiar, round face, he waved his hand vigorously, formed a V with his fingers, and grinned from ear to ear.

The raised hand helped Yoav, who was watching the landing area from another vantage point, to identify Cukurs, memorize his clothes, and pass the vital information to the other team members who had already taken their pre-planned positions.

'Good day, my friend,' I welcomed Cukurs as he finally came through the passport and customs controls. He wore a light suit and a tie, and almost had the look of a respectable businessman.

'I'm so glad to see you.' He shook my hand warmly. 'Greetings from my wife Milda and the children. Tell me what's happening and what's going to happen.'

'Oh,' I replied with a broad smile, 'The best. Believe me, only the best. We have great plans, and you're part of them.'

We got into my black VW, and drove to the centre of Montevideo. Cukurs had no way of knowing that inside the Beetle's trunk my escape suitcase already lay, containing the clothes and necessary papers needed for a hasty exit from the country. I drove in a leisurely and natural fashion. Spy movies tend to depict the driver looking nervously in the rearview mirror, searching for 'tails'. I looked for no 'tails' in the mirror, nor did I drive like a racing-car driver. I drove in the most natural way possible, not wanting to give Cukurs the slightest reason to be tense or concerned.

Cukurs looked pleased. He had already been with me in Montevideo, the previous October, but then he had still been only a candidate for the position, on probation. Now he felt as if he had passed all the tests, and become one among equals, a serious businessman on the verge of a major business breakthrough. With a steady, self-assured gait he walked straight to the reception desk of the Victoria Plaza Hotel.

'Oh yes,' said the reception clerk after consulting the reservations book. 'It says here that Mr Kuenzle has reserved a room for you. Room 1719.' He handed him the key. 'It's a nice and spacious room, sir, and I hope you'll have a pleasant stay with us.'

'Go up to your room, and put your suitcase away. I'll wait for you down here, at the lobby, and look after the car,' I said and smiled to myself as I suddenly remembered that these were almost the very same words I had said to him in October, on our first visit to Montevideo.

Since I couldn't find a parking place, I was forced to double-park in front of the hotel, and the porter, who knew me, made sure that no over-zealous policeman slapped a ticket on my windscreen.

It took Cukurs only a few minutes to settle in his room.

'What a beautiful room,' he commented, not hiding his amazement.

It was indeed a luxurious room in Montevideo's grand hotel, with an exciting panoramic view of the entire city and its vicinity. If he had not realized it until then, then the brief stay in room 1719, paid for by 'Those Who Will Never Forget', made it clear that the age of misery in his life had come to an end and a new era was opening up to him, an era of prosperity and wealth.

'I must go quickly to the Lufthansa office to book our flights. I've arranged quite a tight schedule for us. We've lots of work to do.' I marched briskly to the German airline's office in the building next to our hotel.

The booking clerks there were quite efficient, as usual. I asked to book Cukurs and myself seats on flights leaving for Santiago de Chile. I spoke in a voice loud enough for Cukurs to hear.

'That's settled then,' I said to Cukurs. 'Now, to work. I've already found a place that will serve as our temporary office. I'll show it to you later. It's on our way. But I'm not too happy with the house. It's not elegant, and not sufficiently presentable. I've great plans for some serious investments here, and we'll just have to find a more suitable office.'

We then drove to the Carrasco quarter to inspect a few houses the real-estate agents had lined up for us.

'I'm almost out of petrol,' I pointed out as I merged with the flowing traffic on the promenade. The petrol-gauge supported my assertion, but this too had been pre-planned. Before picking Cukurs up from the airport, I had made sure that the tank was nearly empty, in order to have a plausible excuse to drive into a particular and quite busy petrol station. Dova'le was watching this petrol station, making sure we were on schedule. As I turned into the Texaco petrol station, I noticed the red Beetle parked across the wide street, with Dova'le's silhouette in it, following our every move.

We met with the agent, and went to see some more houses. Following our routine, I let Cukurs conduct the conversations and find out all the details. We visited several houses, and I made sure that everything ran smoothly, without pressure.

'That last one looks quite promising,' I told the agent before parting. 'I like it, despite the price. But I want to think about it some more, and to consult with my partner.' I motioned at Cukurs. 'I'll give you a call tomorrow, and I thank you for your time and your efforts.'

Time was moving on, and we were approaching lunch-time. We said goodbye to the agent, the last non-Israeli to see Cukurs alive and breathing.

'We're really close to the house I rented temporarily. Come, I'd like you to see the place.'

My black Beetle turned slowly into Cartagena Street. The street was quiet. A few hundred metres away I noticed the red Beetle, with our watcher in it. Another Beetle, a green one, was parked closer to Casa Cubertini.

Four or five builders, clad in shabby pants and under-shirts, were working at the next house. They were evidently adhering to the notion that there was nothing in life worth rushing for.

'Here we are. This is the house,' I said to Cukurs.

I came to a halt, turned off the engine, pulled out the key, and got out of the car. Without turning back, I started marching purposefully toward the wooden door of the house.

This is it, I thought, as I walked the last metres to the door. This is the moment of truth. He must follow me now, I reassured myself.

From the corner of my eye I could see Cukurs get out of the car. The sound of the car door closing confirmed the fact that he was behaving exactly as I had predicted. Still walking, I had already pulled the key out of my pocket, and quickly stuck it in the keyhole. Cukurs was 3 or 4 metres behind me.

I pulled the handle, and the white door opened easily inwards.

I entered the house.

The sight that welcomed me was odd, to say the least. Along the walls, making sure not to be detected from outside, stood the members of the team. They were clad only in their underwear. They had taken off their clothes and put them aside in a heap, so that they didn't get covered in blood during the assault.

Cukurs' footsteps could be heard clearly. His well-built figure filled the door frame. He stepped inside. It took him a fraction of a second to become accustomed to the semi-darkness in the room. A fraction of a second too long. I slammed the door behind him with a bang.

The members of the team jumped Cukurs. One of them caught him from behind, in order to execute the single downward blow he had practised for so long. The others leapt at his sides.

Cukurs reacted very fast. Although he was nearly 65, he was in good shape, and the knowledge that this was a life-or-death struggle obviously doubled his strength. He was fighting for his life.

Despite being outnumbered, Cukurs made a few swift movements and managed to shake off his attackers and go for the door. He fought like a wild and wounded animal. He freed one hand, grabbed the door handle, and tried to pull it open. We leaned against the door, trying to push him into the centre of the room. The fear of death gave him incredible strength. During the struggle, he tore the handle right off the door.

'Let me speak,' he yelled. And to this day I wonder why

he yelled in German, and not in Latvian or Portuguese. These were the only words that reverberated in the room. Otherwise we fought silently, without words.

Cukurs' thick-rimmed glasses fell on the floor in the mêlée. Despite the four of us trying to hold him down, Cukurs almost managed to pull the gun out of his pocket. But we beat him to it. We threw ourselves at him, and Yoav let out a quiet cry of pain.

Suddenly someone had a builder's hammer in their hand, and with it hit the Nazi criminal right on his head. Blood spurted everywhere.

The original plan had been to overpower Cukurs, but not to kill him instantly. We had planned on a very brief court martial, in which we intended to read the charges to him, in the name of the 30,000 Jews from Riga and Latvia – children, women, the elderly and men – who had been murdered by him over 20 years ago. We wanted him to know that this entire long affair with Anton Kuenzle and his 'business associates' who came to South America had been designed only to set the stage for the moment of revenge in the name of his innocent victims. And then we were going to put a bullet through his head.

But his attempt to reach for his gun shortened the proceedings. One of us put a gun to Cukurs' head, and pulled the trigger twice. The silencer and the noise of our struggle completely swallowed the sound of the shots. The two bullets ended Cukurs' life. It was Tuesday, 23 February, 1965, 12:30 p.m.

Yoav moaned in pain. During the struggle he had tried to keep Cukurs' mouth shut, to prevent him from calling out for help. With animal instincts, Cukurs bit the hand with all his might. The pain must have been unbearable. Even today, more than 30 years since the struggle at the Casa Cubertini in Montevideo, Yoav still has difficulty moving one injured finger.

The atmosphere in the room was tense. We had no time to celebrate, not even to congratulate one another on the successful completion of our mission.

The voices of the builders filtered in through the windows. They went on with their renovations of the building next door, completely unaware of the struggle that had taken place not 30 metres away from them.

Oswald went out to the yard to turn on the mains, so that we could clean the room and ourselves.

Novelists often describe the last expression in the eyes of the dead, but nothing can be written about Cukurs final stare. His head was smashed, the result of the hammer blow and the two bullets. Blood covered his eyes, ran down his neck, and soaked his shirt.

We pulled his passport out of one of his pockets. A Brazilian alien's passport, No. 27999, issued on 2 February 1965 – two days after I had told him off at the transit lounge of São Paulo's airport. We also retrieved Cukurs' revolver, a small and efficient Italian Beretta, 6.35 mm, model 950, registration number B 78137.

We lifted Cukurs' body and put it in the large trunk with wooden rims and three locks Oswald had purchased. We had to bend the legs of the corpse in order to fit it in. On Cukurs' chest we placed a sheet of paper, with the verdict printed in English, which had been prepared in advance for this historical moment.

> VERDICT
> Considering the gravity of the crimes of which HERBERT CUKURS is accused, notably his personal responsibility in the murder of 30,000 men, women and children, and considering the terrible cruelty shown by HERBERT CUKURS in carrying out his crimes, we condemn the said CUKURS to death.
> He was executed on 23 February 1965
> by 'Those Who Will Never Forget'

We closed the cover of the trunk that had now become Herbert Cukurs' coffin. I could not help but note the irony of history that the Butcher of Riga found his death in the Slaughterhouse Quarter (Carrasco in Spanish).

'We clean and we vanish,' someone said.

We first washed the bloodstains off the walls and floor, then cleaned ourselves up, and put on new clothes. Having made sure that the place was clean and that all our fingerprints had been wiped off the doors and the trunk, we left the house.

Yoav and I got into the black Beetle and left the area. A few minutes later the others followed in the green Beetle. The distant watcher in the red Beetle also disappeared. There were no sounds of screeching wheels or revving engines as everyone drove normally away.

In the nearby house, the builders kept mixing cement, and laying brick upon brick.

16
KUENZLE HERE, KUENZLE THERE

I MANOEUVRED THE car automatically into the centre of Montevideo. I had not yet digested the events of the last hour, putting them aside in some corner of my mind to be raised at a later date with myself, or discussed with someone else.

At the moment I was utterly focused on completing our mission. I made sure to stop at every traffic light and obey every traffic sign, for the last thing I needed now was an uncalled-for encounter with the police.

'Can't you go a little faster?' Yoav pleaded. His impatience stemmed from his swelling finger that had suffered the clamp of Cukurs' strong jaw. I let Yoav off at the Plaza de los Treinta y Tres, drove on for a few more minutes, and parked. I wiped my fingerprints off the steering wheel, the gear shift, and any other part I might have touched. I took my suitcase out of the trunk, and walked away from the black Beetle.

I returned by taxi to the plaza where I had just dropped Yoav, and entered a large café. We had agreed to meet there, all the team members, in order to coordinate our departure from Uruguay.

We looked like a group of businessmen getting together at the end of a regular workday. Not one of the café's patrons could have imagined that only half an hour earlier these five men had killed a sadistic Nazi criminal. Although none of us was a professional killer, we remained absolutely calm and composed, at one with ourselves and our deed, without even a twinge of a guilty conscience. If there was anyone on this earth who deserved to die in such a way and be left in a trunk soaked with his own blood, in an empty room of an isolated house, it was Herbert Cukurs. We felt proud of having had the privilege of taking part in this operation. We only felt sorry that there were not many other operations like this. For we were capable and definitely ready.

'Gentlemen,' Yoav summed up with a few matter-of-fact sentences, devoid of any pathos. 'We've done our job. Great performance. Now we must get out of here safely. Best of luck.'

There were three ways to leave Uruguay: by land, going north to Brazil; by ferry to Buenos Aires; and by air. Naturally we chose the quickest and shortest route.

At Montevideo airport I went to a public phone booth, and called the reception desk at the Royal Plaza Hotel.

'*Buenas tardes.* Anton Kuenzle speaking,' I told the clerk who picked up the phone and knew me well as a regular customer. 'I would like to inform you that neither I nor Señor Cukurs, who's also staying in your hotel, will be returning to the hotel tonight. We had a change of plans at short notice, and are spending the night out of town.'

I could imagine that during our conversation the experienced clerk quickly checked my account, and discovered with relief that Kuenzle and Cukurs' rooms had been paid for in advance, which meant that the hotel wouldn't suffer any financial loss due to our sudden absence. It also meant that there was no reason to be anything but nice toward me. No doubt he said to himself, I wish all the guests were as well organized as this Kuenzle.

'Thank you for letting us know, Herr Kuenzle. Hope to see you very soon.'

The next call was to the Lufthansa office.

'I am very sorry, but a change of schedule forces me for the time being to cancel our reservations to Santiago,' I explained to the booking clerk. 'The names are Kuenzle and Cukurs. Yes, for the flight in two days, on 25 February. I thank you very much, goodbye.'

We, the members of the team, left Montevideo on two separate flights, and of course those who shared the same flight treated one another as total strangers. Only the local Israeli who had served as a watcher remained in town for the time being.

Only when we arrived safely in Buenos Aires did we allow ourselves a modest celebration of our success. We met at a café to coordinate our continued travel arrangements to Europe, and ordered a bottle of champagne.

'I must say that Yitzhak was absolutely right to continuously warn us about The Deceased and his enormous strength. He did not exaggerate at all,' said Yoav and raised his glass with his bandaged hand.

'Yitzhak, I want you to write a letter to the family to put them off track,' he continued. 'I don't want the Cukurs to start looking for the father of the family immediately, or to turn to the police and raise the alarm. We must divert them away from this business.'

On the same day, I sent a letter to São Paulo, written in proper German, and in my neat handwriting, the result of the labour of my dedicated teachers at the German high school in the 1930s. The letter said:

> My dear Herbert,
> With God's help and the assistance of some of our countrymen I made it to Chile in one piece. I'm taking a little rest now after the exhausting journey. I'm sure you too will make your way home very soon.
>
> In the meantime, I found out that we were followed by two strangers, a man and a woman. We must be more cautious and alert. As I told you over and again, you're taking a great risk by living and operating under your real name. Such a risk could be disastrous for us, and also expose my true identity.
>
> Anyway, I just hope that the complications we encountered in Uruguay will serve as a lesson for the future, and that from now on you'll be more careful.
>
> If you detect anything suspicious in your surroundings or your house, do remember my advice – disappear for a year or two among Von Leers' men, until this debate over the Statute of Limitations for Nazi crimes dies out.
>
> The minute you get this letter, please send a reply to Santiago de Chile, to the address you already know.
>
> Yours, Anton K.

Of course we made sure that the letter was sent from Santiago, and that the friend who saw to it also put the appropriate post stamps on it. The letter landed in the Cukurs family mailbox a few days later, by which time all the members of the team had already made it to Europe or Israel.

The Johann Von Leers I had mentioned in my letter was actually one of the top aides to the Nazi propaganda minister, Joseph Goebbels. After the war, Von Leers fled to Argentina and from there, by invitation of the Egyptian government, to Cairo. There he served as special advisor to the Egyptian propaganda minister Abd el Khatem, and was largely responsible for the sharp anti-Semitic undertones that characterized the anti-Israeli propaganda coming out of Cairo at the time. His stay in Egypt was accidentally detected by a British journalist, who was shocked to run into this famous Nazi wandering freely in the Egyptian propaganda ministry. By sheer coincidence, Von Leers died in Cairo only two weeks after I mentioned his name in my diversion letter.

The return to our home bases was quiet and unobtrusive, just as our departure for this operation had been. Apart from our close family members, who were let in on our secret, no one knew about our activities in the previous months.

Being as orderly as I am, I thought it a waste to leave all that money belonging to Anton Kuenzle in the Swiss bank. I had no doubt that once Cukurs' corpse was discovered, it would take the investigators only a short while before reaching this bank account and freezing it. So, the first thing I did after my return from South America was to go to the central branch of Crédit Lyonnais on Boulevard Haussmann. As my friend Oswald watched me from outside, providing security just in case, I went inside and withdrew the thousands of dollars that had remained in the Zurich bank account. From an operational security point of view it was not very wise, but I decided that the risk was negligible, and worth the effort.

Incidentally, in 1996, a fire broke out in the cellar of this bank, completely destroying its entire archives. Among the millions of documents that went up in flames was the receipt for Anton Kuenzle's withdrawal. And so, after a delay of 33 years, the last piece of incriminating evidence of Kuenzle's existence was finally destroyed. This withdrawal was Anton Kuenzle's last act on earth. As I left the bank, the Austrian businessman who had come to life only six months before, had an address and an identity, and had spent months in South America, ceased to exist.

All that was left now was to take care of the media. Having ascertained that all members of the team were safely back, Adi called several news agencies in Germany. He informed them that a Nazi criminal had been liquidated in Montevideo by 'Those Who Will Never Forget' as revenge for the horrors committed by the Nazis against the Jews of Europe, and hung up. We all waited with bated breath for the story to break out in the press and on the radio.

A day passed, then another and another. And still nothing.

We became concerned. What could have happened? How come no one was sent to check the story?

The utter silence most probably stemmed from the combination of journalists' slothfulness and our own lack of experience in such matters. The information Adi passed on to the news agencies must have seemed to lack credibility. We had not taken into account the fact that news agencies are commonly swamped with the weirdest callers promising to expose the strangest and most sensational stories – from encounters with UFOs over Berlin to Nazi abductions in Antarctica. Since the first message we had passed lacked details, the news editors did not bother to go beyond a superficial check. And maybe they had simply been put off by the content of the message. This was the period in which not a week passed without someone discovering Martin Bormann in some remote village in Argentina or Josef Mengele in Nazi-infested Paraguay. It was safe to assume then that the editors found the story unbelievable, and threw it straight into the wastebasket.

'We have no choice. We must lead them to the house in Montevideo,' Yoav decided.

We put everything in writing, all the details of Herbert Cukurs' execution. We provided a full account of Herbert

Cukurs' crimes, the decision to sentence him to death, the precise address of Casa Cubertini in Montevideo, and signed it 'Those Who Will Never Forget'. We sent the story by mail, and followed it up with telephone calls to the news agencies in Düsseldorf, Bonn and Frankfurt.

This time one of the editors must have decided that the new and detailed information was worth a closer examination. He passed the details on to the agency's correspondent in Montevideo. Now it was just a question of time before the entire story became public.

On 6 March, ten days since the last member of the team had closed the door behind him, the wooden door that lacked an inside handle, torn off by Cukurs during the struggle, a police car stopped in front of the small house on Cartagena Street. No one responded to the knocks on the door or to the demands to open it. But the putrid stench emanating from the house convinced the policemen that work waited for them inside.

'We broke into the house through the windows,' reconstructed the senior investigator, Juan Jose Braga. 'A light-coloured bedspread hung a few centimetres away from the entrance, probably to hide the interior of the house that was barren and almost without furniture, except for a few metal beach chairs, wall closets and a brand new electric kettle.'

'On one of the walls we discovered four stains of blood,' Inspector Braga continued his report. 'Each of them was the size of a grapefruit, as if a head had been smashed against the wall several times. On the floor we discovered two bullet cases. A trail of blood led from the centre of the room to the bedroom. There we found a wooden-rimmed, plastic trunk with three large metal locks. The cover of the trunk was closed. There was an unbearable stench in the room. The trunk stood in the middle of an enormous dried pool of blood. There was also blood on the outside of the trunk, and in one place a pool of dried blood had formed. Inside the trunk we found the clothed corpse of an adult male, in the initial stages of decomposition. His head was smashed. His grey hair was soaked with blood. A sheet of paper was attached to the corpse's chest, containing some typed sentences in English. It said that this was the corpse of a man named Cukurs, a war criminal from Latvia, who had been executed by an anonymous group which called itself 'Those Who Will Never Forget'.'

The news of the discovery of the corpse of a Nazi war criminal in a trunk in a deserted house in Montevideo immediately spread throughout the world. From Montevideo to Moscow, from New York to Tel Aviv – large headlines reported the mysterious affair in the small house. Hoards of journalists swarmed around the Carrasco quarter, searching for eyewitnesses and new evidence regarding the corpse and its mysterious killers.

'I noticed nothing out of the ordinary,' said the builder who had worked on the nearby building and who became the media's local hero, pursued by all the journalists who swept through the area. 'I remember that ten days ago some men entered that house. After about an hour they left it as calmly as they had arrived. Two of them left in a black Beetle, and later three others stepped into a green Beetle and drove away. I must stress that their behaviour was completely normal, and there was nothing in their movements to indicate anything out of the ordinary.'

The Uruguayan police weighed up all the possibilities.

'From examining all the facts, we are still not clear whether those strangers wanted to liquidate Cukurs, or had actually planned to kidnap him,' the police investigator related with concern. 'If they only wanted to kill him, they could have hidden the body in one of the cupboards and disappeared. But we found a few items that could indicate kidnapping. For instance, sticky tape, a pair of small scissors, and a pointed metal instrument that could have poked breathing holes in the trunk. The proximity of the house to the sea raises the conjecture that perhaps the killers had planned to move him by boat to one of the ships anchored in the harbour, and then smuggle him out of Uruguay.'

A quick investigation by the harbour police revealed that around the date of Cukurs' disappearance the Israeli freighter *Har Rimon* had anchored in Montevideo harbour. This fact ignited the imagination of several journalists. After all, only five years had passed since Israeli Mossad agents had kidnapped Adolf Eichmann from neighbouring Argentina. They had smuggled him through border controls and brought the Nazi criminal to Israel, where he had been put on trial, found guilty, and sentenced to death. No one paid any attention to the fact that the *Har Rimon* was on a routine commercial voyage, and had reached Montevideo according to a schedule established some considerable time earlier. The announcement by the spokesman of the El-Yam shipping company, the owner of the ship, that the *Har Rimon* had loaded meat, and then made its way to Hamburg via Las Palmas did little to calm the enthusiasm of some Uruguayan journalists who had turned detective, and who claimed that the ship had left Montevideo in a hurry with two mysterious passengers on board.

Newspapers around the world competed with each other in printing new details and facts, all based in part on eyewitness statements, partially on pure conjecture, and partially on wild flights of fantasy.

'In Israeli circles,' wrote the London *Daily Express*, 'the avengers call themselves "The Ones Who Will Never Forget". This is a loosely organized underground of the large and well-organized Jewish community in Argentina.' The British newspaper supported its theory by quoting Yitzhak Rosenberg, the head of Argentina's Jewish Federation, who said, 'It cannot be expected of our people to forget the events of the last war.'

Uruguay's newspapers reported a sensational new theory regarding Cukurs' death, posited by the police investigators. 'Apparently there has been an error in identification. The body found in the Casa Cubertini belongs in fact to a Nazi criminal by the name of Anton Kuenzle.'

The Brazilian newspaper *Anoticia* reported that Cukurs died in an attempt to apprehend Josef Mengele. The paper's correspondent, Elio Tisch, claimed that according to his sources Cukurs intended to hand Mengele over to Jewish agents in return for the promise that he would be allowed to continue to live unhindered in Brazil. Tisch stated that he knew Cukurs personally, and that he also knew that Cukurs had been looking for Mengele in

Paraguay and Brazil. 'There was no intention to kill Cukurs,' Tisch wrote. 'He was murdered by those who know where Mengele is.'

In the meantime, Uruguay's police completed the identification of the corpse. The fingerprints fitted those of Cukurs, and the family of The Deceased identified his clothes and his copper armband. The Uruguayan police began to arrest anyone who had any connection with the affair.

The Greek real-estate agent, Maverides, was detained for two days. Following an intensive interrogation, the investigators finally became convinced that he had nothing to do with it, and set him free.

The San Salvadoran police apprehended two French citizens in San Salvador, Jean-François Retuseau and Jacques-Louis Massiu, whose names appeared on an international arrest warrant issued by the Uruguayan police. The Montevideo investigators decided that the two were connected to the murder since they had arrived in the Uruguayan capital together with Cukurs, on the same flight on Tuesday, 23 February. Uruguay's chief of police, Pablo Puntana, flew especially to San Salvador to interrogate the two. But once again it proved to be a false lead. The two Frenchmen managed to persuade their interrogators that they had never heard of Cukurs, and had absolutely no interest in smashing his skull and shoving him in a travelling trunk. After 48 hours the two were released with an official apology.

The unpleasant turn of events for us was when the State of Israel was dragged into the affair, which led to a diplomatic incident between Israel and Uruguay.

'Interpol has Asked the Help of Israel's Police in Connection with the Assassination of the Nazi Criminal Cukurs,' screamed the headline in the Israeli evening newspaper *Ma'ariv* on 12 March. The subhead stated that Interpol was asking for information and assistance in their search for an Israeli who was involved in the affair. They were looking for the local Israeli who had served as a watcher from a distance of several hundred metres from the house. The Uruguayan police, whose investigators had not handled such a juicy case for years, soon detected his tracks. Well-accustomed to international cooperation, the Uruguayan police asked Israeli police to help find him.

'We don't know his whereabouts,' came the terse reply.

Interpol's investigation request featured not only the name of the watcher, but also my name. It did not take long for the investigators to establish the connection between Anton Kuenzle and Herbert Cukurs. They reconstructed all my moves, paid a visit to my room at the Victoria Plaza Hotel, located the black Beetle I had abandoned in the centre of town, and found out about my connection to Oswald Taussig.

'WANTED' said the headline of Interpol's inquiry form. Copies of the form, with my photograph, were distributed around the world, including Israel. The Interpol document stated that the subject was an Austrian citizen, and mentioned his passport number. A photograph of my friend Oswald also appeared on the form, together with his Austrian passport number.

'Oswald and Kuenzle disappeared without trace on 23 February. Oswald's last recorded act was the return of a rented vehicle, a green VW Beetle. Kuenzle, however, abandoned his black VW Beetle in the centre of Montevideo.' It goes without saying that police attempts to dust these two vehicles for fingerprints proved futile.

Our photographs became quite popular during those spring days of 1965. One of Israel's newspapers printed them along with an explanation that they might be pictures of Joseph Mengele, the Angel of Death from Auschwitz, and another Nazi criminal. The confusion could have been caused by the diversion letter I had sent to Cukurs' address after the mission had been completed.

On 16 March 1965, *Ma'ariv* put Anton Kuenzle's photograph on its front page. The text below it was by the AP correspondent in Montevideo, headlined 'The Mystery Surrounding Anton Kuenzle, "The Smiling Austrian", Wanted In Connection With The Murder Of Herbert Cukurs.'

A weekly magazine in Rio de Janeiro had this very photograph of Kuenzle, 'the smiling man', splashed across an entire page. The picture showed a chubby man, balding, with a moustache, and smiling yet sharp eyes peeping through thick-rimmed glasses. The heavy glasses and thick moustache did little to alter my features, and my friends had no difficulty in identifying me. Neither did my mother-in-law, who remained absolutely silent.

'I have no doubt who murdered my husband,' asserted Milda Cukurs. 'This is the murderer!' she said and pointed at my enlarged photograph. 'My husband told me that if anything happened to him, it would be the sole responsibility of this new friend, this Austrian, this Kuenzle, who sat here, at our home, ate cake and drank coffee with us.'

I smiled when I finished reading the long reports in the Brazilian newspapers. However, I could not help but also think of the danger I had been exposed to for such a long period.

This was close, I realized and heaved a sigh. This was really close, much closer than I had thought at the time.

I thought of all my movements during the preceding months, starting with those early days in September over half a year ago, when I took upon myself the mission, until the moment I leaned hard against the door of the Casa Cubertini to prevent Cukurs, who was fighting for his life, from fleeing.

I had finally managed to win Cukurs' trust and lead him right into the trap, but Milda Cukurs' words only confirmed what I had known and sensed throughout – all along Cukurs and I had been engaged in a life-and-death war of wits.

He had been suspicious of me until the last minute! One mistake, one moment of lost concentration, one accidental slip of tongue, and this entire tale could have had a completely different ending. Cukurs, safe and sound, would have been ensconced in the bosom of his family and continued to fly tourists in his seaplane over São Paulo, while my body slowly decomposed somewhere in a remote banana plantation in the heart of Brazil.

17
THE STATUTE OF LIMITATIONS – ABOLISHED

THE DEBATE over the Statute of Limitations for Nazi crimes was broadcast live on television. The public gallery was packed. The former chancellor, Konrad Adenauer, cancelled all his appointments in order to participate personally in the debate in the West German Parliament in Bonn. Only four days had passed since the Montevideo police investigators had broken into the house on Cartagena Street and discovered the decomposing corpse of Herbert Cukurs. Hundreds of thousands of words were written about this affair throughout the world, and most authors – except for a handful of unrepentant, fanatic neo-Nazis – expressed their full understanding of the motives of 'Those Who Will Never Forget'.

'Only the victims may grant the Nazis clemency,' called Ernst Benda, parliamentary member of the ruling Christian-Democratic Party, who led the struggle against the implementation of the Statute of Limitations on war crimes. Angrily he quoted a letter he had received from a young German, an employee of the Ministry of Justice, who was wondering how the German justice system could put thieves and petty criminals behind bars while despicable murderers were freely walking the streets of Germany, and working in their professions as if nothing had ever happened.

Benda's speech was often interrupted by enthusiastic applause, but also by a few calls of those supporting the Statute of Limitations. These were mainly members of two parties, the Liberal Party and the Christian-Socialist Union Party headed by Franz Josef Strauss. 'It was time to draw a line under the events of the past,' was their main argument.

Minister of Justice Ewald Bucher spoke twice from the podium. As a government minister he admitted for the first time that it was not inconceivable that even after 8 May 1965, criminals and crimes may be discovered that had not been known until then. He then attempted to explain why he personally opposed the change of the law. His opposition stemmed from his concerns that the German justice system might become overburdened, and that miscarriages of justice might occur because the passage of time could render most of the witnesses worthless.

Bucher's remarks drew loud protests from one of his colleagues, Socialist Party member Gerhard Jahn. He reminded the minister of the carelessness with which the judicial system had handled Nazi crimes, and that the prosecutors in the Auschwitz trial had had to visit the Auschwitz and Birkenau concentration camps on their free days and at their own cost, since the state did not see fit to recognize them as work trips.

Public opinion polls showed that most West German citizens opposed the abolition of the Statute of Limitations. As far as they were concerned, it was all over and forgotten. But intellectual circles together with most media outlets pressured for the law to be abolished. The debate in the Parliament became heated. It lasted for seven hours. The photograph of Cukurs' corpse, covered in blood and stuck inside a trunk, with the verdict of 'Those Who Will Never Forget' stuck to its chest, was imprinted in the minds of the participants. I have no doubt that it persuaded some of the floating votes to come down on the side of those who opposed the implementation of the Statute of Limitations. In the decisive vote, most members of parliament decided not to allow the Nazis to benefit from the humane law, and determined that the Statute of Limitations would not be implemented on 8 May 1965, which was the twentieth anniversary of the end of the Second World War and Nazi Germany's capitulation. As a first step, the law was postponed until 1969, and later the Statute of Limitations for Nazi war crimes was abolished altogether.

Following West Germany, other countries, which had been hesitant until then, also decided to continue to hunt down Nazis. Austria, the homeland of many Nazi criminals, which until then had been attempting to avoid confronting its own Nazi past by claiming that it had been conquered by Hitler (Austrian-born himself) in 1938, decided completely to abolish the Statute of Limitations on 16 March. Within just a few weeks many other countries followed suit.

The world decided, and not least due to the operation of 'Those Who Will Never Forget', that there can be no Statute of Limitations and no clemency for criminals like Cukurs.

EPILOGUE: A WAR OF WITS

OVER 30 YEARS have passed since my first encounter with Herbert Cukurs on that beautiful morning at the yacht club on the shores of the lake in São Paulo. I had raised a toast and wished him then a healthy and happy life, which had actually ended in a closed trunk. That was the end of my mission. I returned to Israel, and took a few days off to recuperate and be with my family. My mind was filled with memories, in pictures and in words, thoughts running like a film, impressions from this recent turbulent period as well as from my youth. I often find myself wondering how an ordinary person like myself was capable of thinking, improvising and operating under such extreme pressure. Not that I had had any doubts about my own capacity. I had already withstood many pressured situations, among them special underground operations with the Hagana, one of the pre-state organizations which fought for statehood. Gunfire, mortar shells, heavy gun bombardments . . . none of them were new to me, and I belong to those people who are tense and nervous until the operation begins, when I become utterly calm and composed, and operate in cold blood and with a clear mind.

And yet, this operation was in many respects extraordinary. I operated alone, in a foreign country, where I hardly understood the language, and where I had little influence on the course of events. Even during the most crucial situations I still had to improvise, while being constantly under the suspecting close watch of an opponent who was physically much stronger than I, and whose senses had been sharpened by 20 years of fleeing for his life. He kept looking for the one sign of betrayal, the one false move, the one wrong word, the one unintended gesture. This sadistic mass murderer knew well what fate he deserved. He threw questions at me which no one could have prepared himself for. One mistake, and all my efforts would have been in vain, and I would have vanished without a trace.

My opponent had several assistants – his wife, his children, his daughter-in-law. They served as his antennae, constantly watching me with curiosity and mistrust. He was armed, had a guard dog, and was under the protection of the local authorities.

For a whole month I maintained contact with him. A month of endless possibilities for making the one false move – a word out of place, an odd gesture, a sign of insecurity or inexplicable hesitation. The end of this operation could have been my end.

I passed all the dangers and obstacles. I cannot recall one single mistake, one moment of hesitation or uncertainty. And I cannot help but wonder at this miracle called the human instinct, brain, mind or soul.

And there is one more thing I find quite incredible – although I had put myself in real danger throughout the operation, I had not once felt fear. Only later, when it was all over, did I realize what I had done.

All these experiences had left me with a riddle, which drove me to study psychology in 1977, when I had more time on my hands. But even the sciences did not satisfy my curiosity or provide answers to my questions about the mystery of the soul or the secrets of the human mind. Until today, the human being remains a mystery to me.

When one day my grandchildren ask me, 'Grandpa, of everything you've ever done, what are you most proud of?' I will tell them about my role in this difficult and complicated operation of settling the account with the Hangman of Riga.

Anton Kuenzle